GERMAN HUMOR:
On the Fritz

John Louis Anderson

PERENNIAL LIBRARY

HARPER & ROW, PUBLISHERS, New York
Grand Rapids, Philadelphia, St. Louis, San Francisco
London, Singapore, Sydney, Tokyo, Toronto

For Adaire,
My Best Friend
Who still thinks I am
pretty funny

John Louis Anderson grew up in New Ulm, Minnesota, the most German/ American town in the United States, and was as good a grandson as could be expected to his very German *Oma*, Margaret Strehlau Oas, who lived with his family. He considers being a New Ulmer quite an achievement and takes great pride in it.

Since New Ulm, Mr. Anderson has worked as a photographer and writer for various corporate clients and several national magazines. He is married to Adaire Colleen Peterson, and considers her the best thing that ever happened to him.

Mr. Anderson is the author of *Scandinavian Humor & Other Myths*, the country's best-selling Scandinavian humor book.

The German Gods first appeared in *Mpls/St. Paul magazine.*

Text & Photography: John Louis Anderson
Editor: Sylvia Paine
Cover & Text Design: Tara Christopherson
Editor, Harper & Row: Daniel Bial

First PERENNIAL LIBRARY edition published 1989.

Library of Congress Cataloging-in-Publication Data

Anderson, John Louis.
   German humor : on the fritz / by John Louis Anderson.
     p. cm.
   ISBN: 0-06-096403-0
   1. German Americans—Social life and customs—Humor. I. Title.
  II. Title: On the Fritz.
  E184.G3A53 1989   89-45084
  305.8'31073—dc20

89 90 91 92 93 GP 10 9 8 7 6 5 4 3 2 1

Table of Contents

The New German Gods

One of Germany's leading exports, right behind over-priced luxury cars that explode unexpectedly, is philosophers. Philosophers are people who deal with the great questions of life and death, of man's inhumanity to man, and why modern man can never remember his wife's birthday.

German/Americans, on the other hand, have largely given up the practice of philosophy, because we would have to deal with the great questions of Minnesota, like "Why is there sauerkraut?" or "Is there some *technical* reason why every radio station outside the Metropolitan Mosquito Control District plays only polkas?"

This, of course, leads to the great sociological questions of our age, such as "Why aren't our stations clogged with country-western music like those in the rest of the country?"

Happily, this is one of the few great questions that has a simple answer. Country-western is musical accompaniment for those who want to wallow in self-pity. German/Americans don't believe in wallowing in anything except beer. Besides, self-pity only gets in the way of feeling absolutely certain of yourself and the correctness of your beliefs.

Over the past couple of years, it has been repeatedly, and tactlessly, pointed out to me that Germans, not Scandinavians, are the biggest single population group in Minnesota. I'd like to suggest that people are single for a lot of reasons, including that they can't find a spouse willing to put up with them.

Here then are some guidelines for understanding that largest—and most invisible—of ethnic groups, German/Americans.

BECAUSE!
Gods of Stubbornness

A single god wouldn't do here. There's too much work. German/Americans need a full quartet of gods for this trait, all answering to the family name "Because!" In the rear are "Because I'm the Boss!" next to "Because I'm Your Mother!" They are joined by "Because It's My Baseball!" and his sister "Just Because!"

Some scholars believe that the four gods of stubbornness atavistically relate to the four basic elements of pigheadedness. Actually, German/Americans have four gods of stubbornness because we know we're always in danger of chilling out, of going with the flow, and we need a guardian snit nearby at all times.

You know you're dealing with a manifestation of "Because!" when you run into someone who read the entire dictionary because their spouse once offhandedly criticized their choice of a word.

German/Americans have some wonderful words for unswerving dedication to a task. "Stick-to-it-tiveness," "Dedication," "Thoroughness," "Doing it right" — they all mean exhausting both the topic and yourself; but when you're done, there isn't a drop more blood in that stone.

AEROBIC
Goddess of Compulsions

Germans are great philosophers and can make any notion into an ism. Nudism, as a matter of fact, was a 19th-century German invention. Not Nudism as in "Lying-around-seminaked-at-Club-Med-nudism," but true Teutonic Nudism.

Nineteenth-century German nudists went naked for a Higher Good. They went to the Baltic coast, slept in barracks and rose at 6 a.m. to do calisthenics as the chilly sea fog rolled in. Naked. Because it was *good* for them.

Now that we're Americans and properly ashamed of our bodies, we no longer puff in the buff. But we do other irritating things because they are *good* for us. We jog. We even jog on business trips where no one would know if we slept in. We read the *Wall Street Journal*. We file our recipes on the computer. We have exercise machines in our bathrooms that block the way to the bubble bath. We take educational vacations to places only missionaries used to go. We keep lists of things most people won't even talk about.

Compulsion is just a yuppie version of pigheadedness. Your Uncle August was "set in his ways." You coyly admit to being "compulsive" about some trendy behavior. Guess what your kids will call you.

ZWEI GLAS
God of Beer

Beer is to German/Americans what potato chips are to the rest of the country. We take great pride in not being able to stop at one.

It's amazing that there are still any kidneys and livers left for the University of Minnesota's transplant program.

For German/Americans, beer drinking isn't strictly male behavior. German/American women drink beer with gusto, which shocks newcomers from the coasts. In turn, it shocks Minnesotans to learn that these outsiders consider beer drinking "unladylike." Our feminine ideal is a hearty, laughing waitress capable of carrying eight heavy beer steins, not some simpering ninny barely able to lift her lace parasol.

Beer is the great German Unifier. Catholics drink it. Lutherans drink it. People from every class drink it. Professors and students drink it. Soldiers and pastors, poets and farmers drink it. And every last one of us pretends that our young people wouldn't *dream* of touching the stuff.

German/Americans even think of beer as a health food, to be prescribed for nursing mothers, the pale and sickly, and those staggering under the weight of their own propriety.

German/Americans believe that only an atheist or communist or worse would spread the vicious rumor that there is no beer in heaven. If there isn't, we may have to gentrify purgatory.

BULK
Goddess of Overeating

German/Americans believe in *solid* food! Food with substance! Food with fiber! Food with corners! Food that puts some meat on your bones, and then puts some meat on your meat!

None of this food-as-visual-art stuff. A delicate, translucent broth just means that someone let the chicken escape. A lone asparagus spear on the side of the plate means you forgot the red cabbage.

German/American children think of food as their Duty to their mothers. A Duty is something one does gladly and willingly to keep all hell from breaking loose in the house. German/American mothers give up good jobs downtown to stay home and prepare *proper* meals. Out of Dutiful gratitude for such sacrifice, and concern for their own well-being, German/American children eat like little banshees.

German/American business people are often reluctant to attend business lunches. Raised in the cult of Bulk, they fear that they may lose control in the presence of beefsteak. That sort of enthusiasm might unnerve a new client, particularly a Californian deeply into tofu and bean sprouts.

High school hot lunches and restaurants that consider sauerkraut a vegetable are holy in the cult of Bulk.

EXCOMMUNICATE
God of Absolutes

Germans have always been great philosophers, which seems like quite an achievement until you realize that most philosophy deals with questions like: "How can we *know* that we know the difference between a *house* and a *horse*". Actually, this is a poor example, because it is so practical. Philosophy does not deal with the real world, and neither do philosophers.

German/Americans, on the other hand, have developed many religions that *do* deal with the real world, particularly somebody else's real world. German/Americans view life as a scientific and moral experiment. Somebody else's moral behavior is up for modification, while we serve as the control group.

With such theoscientific certainty behind us, German/Americans see every discussion in absolute terms. We absolutely intend to win the argument. As we see it, you aren't arguing with us, you're defying God.

You cannot win an argument with a German/American, because it matters more to him than it does to you. *Everything* matters most to a German/American.

Only when everything matters can abstract things and ideas matter more than people. Philosopher's Heaven. Peasant's Hell.

ABSOLUTLIG VERBOTEN
God of Rules

If three Germans were stranded on an uninhabited island, they would sit down and elect one of their number mayor. He would appoint the second one chief of police. The third would become bishop. Then they could obey each other till they were rescued.

German/Americans love rules. We especially love rules that are arbitrary, capricious and beyond appeal. This is why German/Americans make such good umpires, grade school librarians and lifeguards.

What's amazing about German/Americans is not just our rule-lust, but that we all *agree* on the rules. Other Americans say they want Law 'n' Order, but can't agree on which laws to enforce. German/Americans believe in keeping order fenced in with a good set of rules. Law is what happens when rules break down and order makes a run for it.

German/Americans don't want to teach the world to sing in perfect harmony; we think the world should already damned well know how!

Absolutlig Verboten lives in the hearts and minds of all German/Americans, the still, tiny voice that says: "What if Father/Pastor/Officer Rolloff finds out...?"

BURGERMEISTER
God of Prosperity

Solid is the only thing that impresses German/Americans. We want a BMW because it's *solid*, not just because it can outrun any Chevy the Highway Patrol can muster. Our food is as *solid* as possible without having to be served in cubes. And we are *solid* enough to drag a 16-disk harrow to the tractor with our bare hands.

Is it any wonder that we consider *solid* a metaphysical goal as well? Our goal is to be known as *solid* citizens. Someone on *solid* ground with the Lord. We want to be people with *solid* marriages, *solid* finances, *solid* reputations.

The veneration of Burgermeister is never more frenzied than at a high school reunion. The competition is not to see who is wealthiest, or even who has had the most babies. The competition (and it is fierce and merciless) is to see who has become the most *solid*.

Other people may compete to see who has become the funkiest since graduation, or may even give a prize for the most outrageous hairdo worn by a 40-year-old. Not German/Americans! Every male in the class gets dressed up in his best suit, like some fool running for county commissioner. Art directors who can't be forced to wear a tie at the office show up in Brooks Brothers suits. Farmers who keep a suit for funerals and the occasional wedding show up in their best basic black.

They're all paying homage to Burgermeister, and the most *solid* among them shall have their names writ large in the book of Republicans.

AUSLANDER
Goddess of Group Cohesiveness

German/Americans aren't exactly tribal, but we've got some small towns that might as well issue their own passports.

Where else could you still be a newcomer after living there for 40 years? Where else could you live, die and be buried, and still be an outsider?

It's not that we don't squabble among ourselves. Put a Commander of the Knights of Columbus in the same room with a Wisconsin Synod Lutheran Congregation President, lock the door, and try to talk about German/American unity. There won't be any until you shove a fellow named Marzetti into the room, and then God help *his* soul.

Much as horses can sense fear, German/Americans have an instinct about outside influences. We can smell a foreign influence on the government at 20 paces, and can spot an outside notion in church at 40.

Nothing short of a tornado can get German/Americans moving as furiously as an outsider trying to mess up our church life. Pity the poor priests who had to celebrate the first mass in English, or the poor pastors who got mixed up in some fool scheme for Nicaragua! Want an open rebellion on your hands? Try dumping the perfectly good hymnals everybody likes and feels comfortable with for some newfangled nonsense.

We only do it because we want to help, because we have more experience, because we know better, because we're older. Besides, who wants their grandchildren to be named Marzetti?

'RAUS!
Goddess of Rudeness

To describe German/Americans as brusquely efficient is like calling the Hell's Angels non-career-oriented. Are you in our way in the grocery store? 'Raus! Are you going too slowly in the left lane of the freeway? 'Raus! Are you standing where we want to be, or in our way in any way, shape or form? 'Raus! 'Raus! 'Raus!

Conservative males fantasize that women are timid and deferential. Obviously these males have never gone grocery shopping on a weekday morning.

Some women may indeed be deferential in the larger, "man's" world, but the supermarkets are *their* turf. Haven't you noticed that the males who work there have to wear camouflage aprons and are as nimble as any ballerina around those panzer carts?

Supermarkets can be an antifeminist's vision of hell, with pushy women pushing carts into everything in their path. The very deepest levels of this hell are filled with German/American women. German/American women know no fear.

We German/Americans don't see ourselves as rude. We see ourselves as forthright. We will forthrightly, and with all good will, tell you that you should change your hair style, lose weight or wash your shirt more often. The second time we meet you, we will give you even more good advice.

ORDER
God of Tidiness

When Germans sing "We Are the World," it makes a lot of people uncomfortable. And just because Germans are so tidy!

Life would be so appealing if there were no untidy litter. No untidy thoughts. No untidy people. But if you think a woman's work is never done...

Happily, German/Americans lack that sort of evangelical tidiness. But we've still got enough of the bug to make life stressful. Consider Otto and Theresa Hofstein, for example. Otto and Theresa have divided their lives into clearly marked zones — his car, her kitchen; his recliner, her silverware; and so on.

Otto is very proud of that car, and it shows. You haven't seen a 1972 Buick that looked so good since Richard Nixon was President.

But the seats were just plain ragged! Theresa figured it might be *his* car, but chairs were *her* responsibility, and those car seats were a *terrible* reflection on her!

So when Otto went fishing with Red Geisthardt, Theresa went out and made the nicest slipcovers you've ever seen.

Of course, when Otto got back with no crappies and a bad attitude, he wasn't in any mood to see paisley seats in the Buick.

What saved this marriage was Otto's Germanic sense of Order. Now the '72 is *her* car. *His* car is an '89 Mazda RX-7. And there are no damned slipcovers in it!

HOOLEREI
Gods of Outstate Radio

It's frightening how much you can learn about an area just by driving through it. Drive through industrial New Jersey and learn about graffiti. Drive through the deep South and learn from road signs where your soul is headed. Drive through Minnesota and learn how hard it is to tell one polka from another.

In Minnesota, the billboards may say, "Lena loves butter better than Ole," but all you'll hear on your car radio is polka. Don't feel bad if you can't tell "The Little Miss Polka" from "The Jolly Farmer Polka" from "The Petunia Stomper Polka."

One of the great secrets of our time is that there is only one polka. It was recorded in 1947 by "Whoopee" John Wilfahrt, and it lasted nine hours. Ever since then, radio stations in southern Minnesota have been playing seven-minute segments of that same polka. Some stations even have it on an endless tape loop, interrupting it only to give hog prices.

The framers of the U.S. Constitution wisely put certain things beyond the vote of the people, like the Bill of Rights and the selection of a national anthem. If we ever voted on a new anthem, the German/Americans would vote as a bloc, and we'd have to start ball games with a polka.

KITSCH
God of Sentimentality

We German/Americans are not well known for our sense of irony, because we are conserving it for the greatest irony of all: Teutonic Sentimentality.

Beneath our steely Teutonic carapace lies the world's largest-known deposit of gush and goo. Men with the competitive instincts of a great white shark leave it all at the office and go home to gently tend their cuckoo clocks. Women with a stare flinty enough to crack ice cubes turn into kittens around their Hummel figurines.

Sentimentality is a refreshing break from our usual brutal honesty. We're continually Facing Up to the Facts or, more enjoyably, making someone *else* Face Up to the Facts. *Ehrlichkeit am Jeden Preis!* Honesty at Any Price!

Yet what is sentimentality but love without honesty? No wonder we find it so restful and seek it so desperately. It's our only respite from Honesty at Any Price, and from the responsibility of living up to other people's expectations.

For all I know, Arnold Schwarzenegger collects Steiff teddy bears.

26

Lifestyles of the Strong and Certain:

A True or False Quiz

Germans are the biggest ethnic group in America, but it's generally easier to get them to pick up the check at the restaurant (wildly un-Teutonic behavior) than to openly admit that they're German.

I don't know why this should be. Everybody in America (except Detroit) wants to have a German automobile. We feel safer when we're flying on an airplane serviced by a German maintenance team. And we all want the people who work for us, whether it's our lawyers or our employees, to have that Teutonic tenacity and work ethic. German/Americans see workaholism as a social norm, not a failing.

You know you work in a German/American office if nobody takes coffee breaks, everybody eats lunch at their desks, and the office Christmas party is just another networking opportunity.

You know your neighbors are German/American if their grass is always perfect, and their dog and children all heel.

But how do you know if *you* are German/American? Rather than lie awake nights trying to deduce it through logical analysis (a sure sign of Germanity), just take this test.

Because all of life is either True or False for German/Americans, this test is a True or False test. Arguing about how the questions are phrased will cost you points. Using phrases like "Sometimes..." or "On the other hand..." smacks of situation ethics and will get you disqualified.

Answer every question. You have 12 minutes.

Do You Qualify as a German/American?

You will answer all these questions either TRUE or FALSE. There is no room for equivocators among German/Americans.

1. _____You will go bankrupt unless you hammer every used nail till it is straight again.

2. _____The word "interactive" is O.K. when it refers to machines or video games, but not when it refers to children.

3. _____Everyone should subscribe to at least three news magazines, in order to compare and contrast coverage of the same news event.

4. _____People with no money in the bank are no better than people on welfare.

5. _____People who look forward to vacations are probably not good employees and should be watched.

6. _____USA Today is for people who think TV news shows are always getting bogged down in details.

7. _____The three dirtiest words in the English language are Lazy, Late and Liberal.

8. _____Every schoolchild ought to learn English, German and at least one foreign language.

9. _____Everyone should have a printed schedule for vacuuming the lint out of their hair dryers.

10. _____Everyone should be able to give you the dates of their dental checkups for two years in advance.

11. _____Everyone should memorize not only their Social Security number but the numbers of their health care policy, auto insurance policy and driver's license.

12. _____God listens more closely when you sing "Stille Nacht" in German than in the English translation.

13. _____Everyone should vacuum not only the back-seat floor but the trunk of their car every week.

14. _____In order to be fully prepared, all German/American women, even the ones who deny it, have at least one little fold-up plastic rain cap.

15. _____Everyone should label and file all the buttons they get with a new shirt or blouse. These buttons should be cross-indexed as to color and fabric. Notes should be kept on which garment they go with, its cost and place of purchase.

16. _____Everyone should give all their old clothes to Goodwill, even the ones street people wouldn't wear.

17. _____If a shirt is actually torn in half, you should cut off all the buttons, file them, and make dust rags out of the cloth.

18. _____New daughters-in-law will treasure these dust rags because they're so sensible (both the daughters-in-law and the dusters).

19. _____Everyone should buy an expensive beer stein when they go to Germany, whether or not they can read the German on it.

20._____ If they are liberals, they may not *want* to have their stein translated.

21. _____Translating the stein and making them Face Up to the Facts would be a *very* German thing to do, though.

22. _____True courage is based on the ability to Face Up to the Facts without flinching.

23. _____German/Americans may be tough when Facing Up to the Facts, but they're not masochists. They'd much rather make somebody *else* Face Up to the Facts.

24. _____German/Americans do not have a drinking problem. They are the upholders of a millennia-old tradition.

25. _____Group tours of foreign countries, particularly those countries where the road signs are not properly maintained, are a wise and jolly thing to do.

26. _____Taking a group tour to Germany, however, suggests a lack of mental toughness and resourcefulness.

27. _____Mexico is a wonderful place to travel because the music sounds so much like polka.

28. _____A poorly weeded garden is the first sign of Alzheimer's.

29. _____No garden is complete without plaster deer, elves, geese or "Fannies."

30. _____The best way to travel by car is to have the women all sit in the back seat, with the men up front.

31. _____A messy farmyard is an absolute sign of an incompetent farmer.

32. _____People who don't mow their lawns are probably on drugs, or welfare, or both.

33. _____Looking at dirty pictures will make you a serial killer.

34. _____Teenage necking leads inevitably to pregnancy.

35. _____Marijuana always leads to heroin.

36. _____Farm loans lead only to poverty.

37. _____Spending money causes insanity.

38. _____Most of the world's woes come from people who get excited about any- and everything.

39. _____New York City is full of people who actually believe that Geraldo Rivera is a respectable journalist.

40. _____There is no problem so big that it couldn't be solved by putting you in charge.

41. _____You and your friends are the only people around here who are doing your jobs 100 percent.

42. _____Actually, you're doing 150 percent because you have to do everybody else's job too.

43. _____The word "lifestyle" should be banned because it isn't *precise*.

44. _____It is appropriate and caring for someone to ask a new mother publicly how her milk production is coming.

45. _____If a new mother drinks enough good German beer, she will have better milk production for her baby. (The baby will be less fretful as well.)

46. _____People who do whatever pops into their heads never amount to much in life.

47. _____The main problem with the game "Dungeons and Dragons" is that it is only a fantasy.

48. _____Young urban males who drive jacked-up pickups with outsized tires have already peaked and will spend the rest of their lives listening to re-releases of today's pop music.

49. _____People with vanity license plates are shallow show-offs who probably have dead-end jobs and several child-support payments to make.

50. _____A man who does not drink beer is probably a security risk.

SCORING: Why are you asking us? You know who you are!

Nothing is more important to German/Americans than family tradition. Elfriede Unterguttenberger is credited with having created the Unterguttenberger family motto in 1752 — "Passion Is for People Who Can't Polka."

The Unterguttenbergers have treasured this wisdom from their ancestor for over two centuries now, even though it had little relation to reality. The Unterguttenbergers have excelled in both polka *and* passion, with an average of 17 children per family well into the 20th century.

Duty, Hard Work and Tidiness:

Life Among German/Americans

Not many young people today remember that great old German/American kiddie TV favorite, "The Howdy Duty Show." Not the later Americanized version with the dorky puppet and Buffalo Bob, but the original show, telecast live daily from Milwaukee's *Howdy Volks Theatre*.

We children would gather (in tidy rows, of course) around the television set and watch enthralled as Howdy explained life in terms we could understand. Everything in life, he would say, is Duty. Duty is what makes life enjoyable. When faced with a duty — washing dishes, mowing the lawn, weeding 10 acres of cabbages — we shouldn't cringe and whine and desert our posts. We should walk right up to the task, stand up tall, wave and say "Howdy, Duty!"

The powerful influence of this show may explain a lot of our later behavior. We believe in Duty. We believe that everyone has a duty to do. We further believe that it is our duty to make sure they do their duty properly.

We believe in hard work. A lot of us enjoy hard work because it brings a sense of accomplishment. The rest of us only work hard in order to bitch about everybody we think isn't working as hard.

We believe in tidiness. We mow our lawns once a week, even during droughts. We have our opinions trimmed once a week at church. And whenever our hair grows down or our shrubs grow up, we snip them close to the source too.

In short, we're an amazingly organized, orderly people. We make our lists, and then we live by them. Who cares if that sometimes makes life as dull as a computer manual? We're just following orders.

New Old German Folk Wisdom Sayings for Our Time

The folk wisdom of a people is contained in its proverbs. Unfortunately, these proverbs are usually expressed in some archaic folk language that only graduate students can still understand.

What we need are Old-Time Proverbs that speak to our modern lives. Not obvious stuff, like "Don't lend money to junkies," but folk wisdom for an age of historical miniseries.

I can vouch for the authenticity of these Old German Folk Wisdom Sayings because I grew up in New Ulm, Minnesota, I'm part German, and the German side of me just made them up.

I know they're old wisdom because it's Monday morning, and frankly, I never expected to feel like this until I was about 114.

Old German Proverbs for Our Time:

Children are a blessing you may not have asked for, but if you complain, God will give you something even worse.

Plant your crops early;
But not too early.
Go to bed early;
But not too early.
Get up in the middle of the night;
And get back to work.

A fat cat and a thin wallet are sure signs that your pets are embezzling.

If you do not treat your wife with respect, she will feed you many meals with mashed potatoes and you will get fat and die.

Every dog has its day, but there will be a handling charge.

Guard your tongue until granted full immunity.

The Good Lord will always provide, even if you have to go to court to get a settlement.

Guard your reputation, for it is all that you have, unless you own most of the farmland in the county.

A little polka never hurt anyone, but the Klopfen dance can break your leg if your neighbor hates you.

A mother should not worry about her son's path through life unless he wants to be a game show host.

A preacher proclaims what he does not know. A politician promises what he cannot do. A bully threatens what he does not dare. But the phone company *will* cut off your service if you don't pay.

Always speak the truth, but leave yourself a way out.

Regularity is the secret ingredient for peace of mind.

Old friends are best, but the new ones don't know what a rat you can be.

Passion is for people who can't polka.

A young man wants macrobiotic cold cereal and a hot wife. An old man wants hot porridge and a warm comforter. Middle-aged men want a hot wife and get cold comfort.

God made men stronger than women so they could work hard and die in the fields.

Any man who thinks God did him a favor by making him the head of the family should remember what body part most often gets shot off in war.

When you are with bakers, talk bread. When you are with butchers, talk sausage. When you are caught in the middle, talk sandwiches.

A housecat that won't mouse is probably a vegetarian New Age crystal freak.

Only an old fool or a new parent thinks children will always obey.

Beer may be better than blood, but you need fewer transfusions.

A daughter is a daughter all her life long, unless she has a sex-change operation.

Save your money, be frugal and invest wisely. Then watch the weird kid next door become a millionaire rock star.

Don't think you're so good! Heaven is never more than a stone's throw away from Hell.

Never judge a man by one thing. If he doesn't do everything perfectly, he's a bad man.

Never loan money to a baker if his only collateral is sauerkraut.

It doesn't matter how much you make, just what you've got saved in the bank.

43 Fun Things You Ought to Do That You'd Really Rather Not

Everybody has a little job list. Mow the lawn, clean out the closets, and so on. German/Americans have *already* mowed the lawn and cleaned out their closets, so their lists are a little more ambitious. And compulsive. What's unique about German/Americans is that they don't automatically shout "Forget it!" when they're confronted with choices like these.

1. Make a proper compost heap with the grass clippings you get when you mow the lawn every week.
2. Volunteer to take 20 Cub Scouts on an overnight trip.
3. Take a course to brush up your accounting skills before next tax time.
4. Visit your family more often. Be nice to your sister's husband.
5. Landscape your back yard. Move shrubs around. Get rid of that stump. Widen your driveway.
6. Discuss where you think your relationship is going with your spouse. Compare and contrast the strengths and weaknesses you've become aware of since your first child. Use flip charts if necessary.
7. Preview *all* your child's TV shows. Take out seven or eight video tapes on Bargain Night. Take notes on socially inappropriate behaviors. Discuss them all with your child before you let him/her watch the tapes. Discuss the child's reaction after seeing the tape.
8. Alphabetize and catalogue your tapes, CD's and record albums.
9. Enter your stray recipes into your computer. Then organize your grocery coupons.
10. Label all your snapshots and put them in an archival scrapbook.
11. Take everything you haven't used in the past three years to Goodwill.

12. Check under your sink and put Mr. Yuk stickers on everything dangerous, even if your kids are in college.
13. Review your family's fire-emergency exit plans.
14. Photograph everything you own for insurance purposes.
15. Study a non-European language for a year to broaden your horizons.
16. Read two of the Great Books of Western Civilization you've been promising to read ever since college.
17. Form a better self-image.
18. Spend a minute to think what your household furniture is saying about you. Make any necessary corrections.
19. Confront the office gossip.
20. Take time to be someone's friend.
21. Throw out your old *National Geographics*.
22. Hold a garage sale. See if anybody wants to buy a bunch of old *National Geographics*.
23. Send away for a map from the Environmental Protection Agency and see if you live near a toxic waste dump.
24. Rotate your tires, and check your automobile's fuses.
25. Check your cabinets for formaldehyde fumes, your basement for radon, your ceilings for asbestos, your refrigerator for PCB's, your tap water for lead, your lawn for pesticides, your kitchen for gas fumes, and your whole house for carbon monoxide. Try not to panic.
26. Read all about Lyme disease so you can recognize the symptoms from the bugs you can't even see.
27. Familiarize yourself with your community's Civil Defense plans. Learn all the evacuation routes, and drive them several times to familiarize yourself with them.
28. Memorize the names of all 61 Vice Presidents of the United States so you can recite them sometime as a party gag.
29. Check the entire family's underwear, and replace any weak elastic.
30. Wash all your socks at one time. Spread them out on the living room floor so you can perfectly match them for length, texture and color.

31. This winter, give your lawnmower a thorough tune-up.
32. Write *real* letters to all the people on your Christmas list. Tell only the truth and don't draw attention to yourself.
33. Paint your living room again. Then paint the bedrooms. Just don't go getting wild on the colors.
34. Finish that craft project. Start one if you haven't recently, and see it through to the end.
35. Think of how different your life would have been if you had married someone else (*you* know who!). Make a list of pros and cons for your current spouse. Burn list immediately.
36. Clean out your refrigerator. Combine half-filled jars of pickle relish. Arrange the jars of mustard, relishes and salad dressings so that those closest to their expiration dates are up front.
37. Clean out your spice cabinet. Forget to tell your spouse what you did until he or she is busy cooking some special, exotic meal.
38. Research and prepare a private position paper comparing and contrasting socialism as practiced in Burma, Sweden, Yugoslavia, and any three African states chosen at random. Ask to present your findings to the local Rotary club.
39. Plan next summer's garden, and make up your weeding schedule. Put some teeth in this resolution so there are consequences.
40. Compare the decor of your home with the photos in *Architectural Digest*. Ask yourself where you went wrong. Ask yourself where *they* went wrong.
41. Invite the ladies with the *Watchtower* pamphlets into your house, so you can share your deepest religious beliefs with them.
42. Take the S.A.T. Test (or even the G.R.E.) again, to see if you have gotten intellectually lazy since you were in school.
43. Write your Christmas cards on your vacation, so you won't waste all that time sitting around the beach.

The Tao of Tools for German/Americans

Lots of people don't give much thought to anything, let alone to the philosophical side of power tools. German/Americans, on the other hand, give a lot of thought to *everything*, including tools.

We realize that tools are a metaphysical extension of the self: Inanimate objects that tell the world about the *persona* of the user, that speak of that person's highest aspirations, and probably even hint darkly at the lengths to which that person is willing to go to *get* it.

You can better understand German/Americans by considering what tools perfectly embody our world view and our approach to problem-solving. Consider these tools as philosophical guideposts to the German/American psyche:

1. **Biofeedback.**
   (Who else would turn to a machine to help them explore their own bodies?)
2. **All-Terrain Vehicles.**
   (What fun is something unless it's a *little* invasive?)
3. **Chain Saws.**
   (If Nietzsche had gone to Walden Pond...)
4. **Indoor/Outdoor Thermometers.**
   (Particularly if they are digital and in Celsius.)
5. **Computer-generated Art.**
   (It's no coincidence that Max Headroom is blond.)
6. **Fishing Sonar.**
   (Considered sporting by those who use depth charges for bait.)
7. **World Maps with Clocks Showing the Time Around the World.**
   (How can you keep track of people if you don't know when they're sleeping?)
8. **Pedometer.**
   (Strap it to your leg and turn a stroll in the moonlight

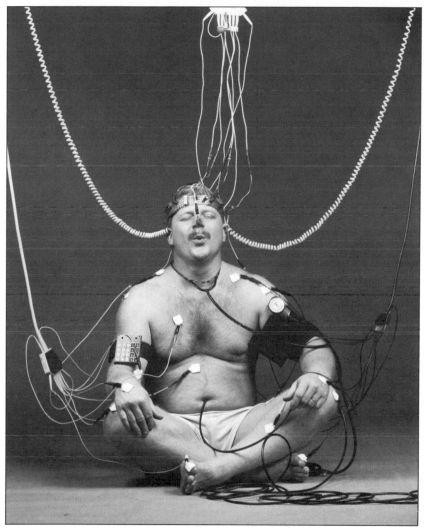

BIOFEEDBACK: *The Newest Management Tool?*
Bill Nietzsche has taken the concept of biofeedback one step further
into a Bio-MIS (Management Information System). Bill is now marketing
his BMIS system to executives who want to push themselves to their
limits of productivity while also keeping track of the most secret parts of
their employees' lives. "This is better than drug testing and lie detectors
combined," says Mr. Nietzsche. "I mean, this software gets right down to
your people's *attitudes!*"

into a quantifiable experiment.)
9. **"An *Entire...*" Collection of Anything.**
(Why settle for a hint when you can have an encyclopedia?)
10. **Perfectly Catalogued and Labeled Photo Albums.**
(In 200 years, the museum will be grateful for all the names and dates.)
11. **Tractor Pulls.**
(Why waste all that power on soybeans?)
12. **Bulldozers.**
(Built to remedy those things — e.g., trees, hills, walls— that are not where they belong.)
13. **Trivial Pursuit as a Blood Sport.**
(If Scrabble players have an official dictionary, why shouldn't you be able to bring along an encyclopedia to prove you're right?)

The Teutonic Tourist:
Vacations as Learning Experiences

German/Americans see no reason to lose your grip on yourself just because you're on vacation.

Vacations are not for lollygagging around on some beach, getting drunk. That's what the State Fair is for, and there you don't have to worry about skin cancer.

No guilt is greater for a German/American than Gold Guilt. It's sinful to waste money on a vacation for which you don't have to study, or one that doesn't cause you some discomfort. If you ever see a blond curled up in a fetal position on a Caribbean beach, it's only a German/American hallucinating a lecture from his father about the value of a dollar.

He won't be back in Cancun next year. He'll spend his vacation building homes for the homeless, or working on a small-scale hydroelectric power project in the Sudan. But he won't be a haunted man, and he will have accomplished something!

What Makes a Vacation Meaningful for German/Americans?

1. German/Americans prefer to vacation in places where, till recently, only missionaries used to go.
2. German/Americans love organized vacations. Organized to the point of scheduling rest stops on the itinerary is best.
3. German/Americans love to visit ruins, because then they must study the entire culture that left those ruins and formulate their own hypothesis on that society's fate. They enjoy, even expect, to be quizzed by the guide when they get back on the bus.
4. German/Americans expect to *learn* something from their vacations, like how many metric tons of stone were carved in Machu Picchu, or how many man-hours were required to construct the Great Wall. What fun is seeing a pyramid in the jungle if you don't know how much it weighs?
5. German/Americans love being *methodical* on vacation. If they come home with a tan, you know they went at it *methodically*, with six different sun blocks, a chart and probably a stopwatch.

Ideal Domestic Vacations for German/Americans:

1. Participate in a herpetological expedition in Death Valley.
2. Go whitewater rafting down the Colorado River through the Grand Canyon.
3. Take any museum-related tour, particularly one where you serve as an unpaid assistant at an archeological dig.
4. Stay busy, busy, busy! Nobody has more activities and programs for busy campers than Club Med.

At a chance meeting of representatives of the First and Third worlds, the outstanding concern for the representative of the Third World was in correcting a particularly troublesome snuggie.

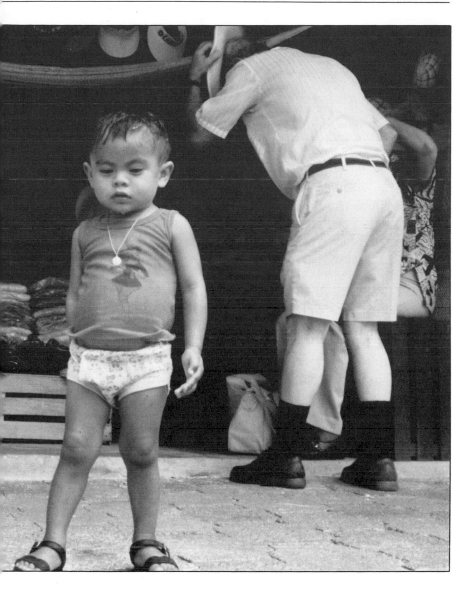

5. Serve as a camp counselor at a Boy Scout, Girl Scout or church camp. You can organize their little lives from 6 a.m. reveille to 10 p.m. collapse.

Ideal International Vacations for German/Americans:

1. Take the Grand Mayan tour — Palenque, Uxmal, Chichén Itzá, Cobá and Tikal.
2. Go to Easter Island by tramp freighter.
3. Raft the Zambezi River from Victoria Falls to Lake Kariba.
4. Tour China by bicycling from Beijing to Tibet.
5. Sign on to participate in a whale census off the coast of Antarctica.

The Ultimate German/American Vacation:

Every fall, the 750 tribes of New Guinea hold a huge gathering called a Sing-Sing. German/Americans who manage to take a boat up the Sepik River or fly into the site in a small aircraft may think they have gone to Teutonic Tourist Heaven.

Consider:
1. New Guinea is practically the only place in the Third World with Lutheran churches.
2. It is easier to learn the local language — Pidgin — than it would be to learn Farsi or Mandarin Chinese.

Good and Bad Jobs for German/Americans

German/Americans like jobs in offices large enough to require a map. If the office map itself is classified, they're practically orgasmic.

German/Americans think a job, like life, ought to have structure. They don't necessarily lust to be on the top of that structure. They just want *in*! Structure is its own reward.

German/Americans enjoy carrying out orders as much as they enjoy giving them. It's all part of the structure.

German/Americans like jobs that have dress codes. Nobody wants to be seen with a bunch of people who have their shirts untucked.

German/Americans have particularly liked jobs that require a uniform. Scientific researchers, doctors and nurses get to wear lab coats, police get to wear tight blue shirts and heavy shoes, and now the U.S. Army has a helmet that looks like it came out of an old John Wayne/Audie Murphy movie.

As soon as German/Americans realize that ice cream wagon drivers wear uniforms, they'll do a leveraged buy-out of the industry and really shape things up. *Then* you'll see that bunch of 5-year-old slackards waiting in a (straight) line with exact change — *or else!*

The reason German/Americans study hard to become experts in their fields is so no one can argue with them.

Good Jobs for German/Americans

German/Americans really lust after jobs like these. Particularly the jobs that come with epaulets you can wear on your pajamas.

1. Small-town police chief — There's no civilian review board here, unless you arrest someone on the Chamber of Commerce for speeding.
2. Credit manager — Only God and loan officers answer to no one for their decisions.
3. Bishop — It doesn't matter whether it's Catholic or Lutheran — you've made your mother proud of you.
4. Aerobics or drill instructor — The only difference is color. D.I.'s dress in olive drab, but there's no telling what color an aerobics instructor will wear.
5. Anything at the Pentagon — This is Valhalla! A German/American paradise complete with uniforms and orders to follow, where everything is classified and no one is ultimately responsible.
6. Librarian — Being a librarian is the most civilized way of

telling people to shut up, as well as telling them what they may and may not read.

7. Lifeguard — Where do they get these people with perfect bodies and no sense of humor?

8. Spokesman for the National Rifle Association — No sense pussyfooting around when you know you're right. If they're scared of you, so much the better.

9. Civil Defense director — Whatever it is that a Civil Defense director does between summer tornados and spring floods, he gets to do it wearing his Civil Defense helmet.

10. Anything in a lab coat — Doctors have power over us ("No more cholesterol or smoking for you, Mr. Priebe"), and lab technicians know our secrets ("Hey guys — Mrs. Gruenenfelder's pregnant. Again."). And then there are dentists...

Bad Jobs for German/Americans

German/Americans believe that there is *no* job that a German/American can't handle better than anyone else, given the proper training, organizational support and discipline. There's no sense even talking about what we couldn't do.

While there are no jobs German/Americans can't do, there are some for which they believe other people are better suited.

1. Pit man at the Chicago Board of Trade — Or any job where you can't tell people to shut up.

2. Sensitivity trainer — Or any job where the boss wants to be your pal.

3. Community arts administrator — Or any job where the organizational chart is made up entirely of dotted lines.

4. Public relations person at a corporate takeover target — Or any job that requires keeping the media and the public informed and happy *every single day!*

5. Complaint-department representative — Or any job where you have to suffer fools, gladly or otherwise.

6. Freelance anything — Or any job where you make up the

rules as you go along.
7. Child-care worker at a holistic day-care center — Or any "non-authoritarian" job. (Warning: If your boss is German/American, "non-authoritarian" just means that the boss is willing to let you make up your own mind to do what he/she wants you to do.)
8. Amway sales representative — Or any job that promises to help you fulfill your full potential for self-actualization.

Heaven Is a German/American Auto Mechanic

German/Americans raise workaholism to the level of a cultural norm. Experts are divided on whether this trait is genetic or viral.

Let's just say that there are certain jobs that the rest of us *want* to see German/Americans holding down.

1. Airline maintenance and inspection
2. Lawyer (*our* lawyer, that is)
3. Accountant
4. Auto mechanic
5. Anybody employed by us

Hell Is a German/American IRS Auditor

Keep your passport up-to-date and your tank full of gas. You could someday find yourself having a little chat with one of these nightmare figures.

1. A German/American IRS agent looking for a promotion
2. A German/American county attorney running for re-election
3. A German/American investigative reporter from "60 Minutes"
4. A German/American savings and loan auditor on a surprise visit
5. A German/American traffic cop whose spouse had a headache last night.

Wilhelmina Weidenschlagen has been giving advice for so long now that she has become something of a performance artist.

She claims never to have heard of the phrase, "Mind Your Own Business," and thinks that "Just Say No" is too short-winded to qualify as good advice.

"About Your Hair...":
Speaking the Truth, Regardless

Nobody is better at speaking the truth than German/ Americans. We view it as a sort of public service. We don't think it's rude to walk up to someone to whom we've only recently been introduced and tell them honestly that their hair style doesn't flatter their full figure and face. For all you know, they may not have *noticed!*

Other people wait till your clothes are on fire before they violate your private space — before they make demands on you. We think that is uncaring. It is unhelpful. If God has given us the ability to see right from wrong, then God has put us here to set right what is wrong in the world. To deny this would be to tread the boundaries of blasphemy.

What continually astonishes us is the ungenerous reception we so often receive. I've gone to the trouble of asking a number of people about their experiences with German/Americans. They *all* seemed to have lots of examples. The more German/ Americans they knew, the more examples they had!

Orders from Your Mother:
When Your Children Lack the Courage of Your Convictions

We German/Americans are always generous with our advice, but never so generous as with our own families. We consider advice the byproduct of our years of experience, to be passed on to the younger generation. But like any byproduct, it sometimes turns a little toxic. In fact, the generation gap can sometimes grow into a major landfill.

Here's a little look at how similar your family probably is to everybody else's family. Ain't love grand to be able to overlook stuff like this?

Advice on Romance, Sex and *That* Stuff:

"My parents had only three rules, and they applied to all areas of my sister's and my life:
1. DON'T DO IT! If we were already doing it,
2. STOP IT!! And if we didn't,
3. YOU NEVER LEARNED BEHAVIOR LIKE THAT AROUND THIS HOUSE!!" — *Banker*

"Parents tend to give contradictory messages about sex. The basic message too often is 'Sex is filthy and disgusting, so you ought to save it for the person you'll marry.' "
— *Family counselor*

"My mother could never actually bring herself to talk about sex. She just opened my mail, went through my wallet, turned both mattresses in my bed over weekly, and used a nail to pick the lock on the bathroom door when I was in there too long for her taste.

"Then she would critique my past week. If she was feeling particularly good, she would also cry and quote me Bible verses. She had an old Bible that zipped shut, just like her mind."
— *Administrative assistant*

"My mother told me, 'Never do anything you would be ashamed to do in the Boston Public Garden at noon.' I guess she thought that would keep me pretty good, but I just made up my mind that if I wanted to do anything, I'd better be prepared to do a show-and-tell on it sometime. It actually made romance more exciting!"
— *Teacher*

"I have been a disappointment to my mother all my life. First, I did not go into the priesthood. Then I married a Norwegian Lutheran, who did not convert. A blue-eyed Norwegian, I might add.

"Last year, Carol and I adopted a Korean baby. I thought she'd be thrilled, but she was apparently still in shock about having to set a place for a Norwegian at Thanksgiving. So I told her, 'Mom, it ought to make you happy that every one of your grandchildren has brown eyes.' "
— *Foreman*

"My mother never gave advice. She spoke the truth. The truth, according to her, was that I wasn't pretty enough, vivacious enough, smart enough or religious enough. I grew up thinking that truth is something you use to hurt people."
— *Teacher*

"At a family picnic when I was in sixth grade, my mother screamed at me 'Don't you *dare* go into the woods with Jimmy! He's your third cousin!'

"It was *years* before I understood why that was supposed to be bad, and then I found out that she thought I would debauch that little creep, Jimmy."
— *Dentist (female)*

"My father was a farmer who went to bed immediately after the 10 o'clock weather. But on the night before my wedding, he stayed up till I was safely tucked in bed. I can only assume he was guarding my last 24 hours of virtue.

"After I was married, my mother suddenly became obsessed with my nutrition. Every time she called, she asked if I was getting enough fresh fruits and vegetables (this from a

Greta Geiselbrechtinger monitors four newspapers daily to discover new dangers so she can warn her grandchildren and make them do what's safe.

woman with less nutritional training than a short-order cook).

"I can only assume that she was afraid that since I had strayed from the straight and narrow by marrying Charlie, I would inevitably stray from my major food groups as well."

— *Counselor*

"My mother and father used to solemnly assure me that dirty jokes came from men in prison, who apparently had the time on their hands to come up with such terrible things. I believed that wholeheartedly, particularly when we drove by the prison at Sandstone.

"But they overplayed their hand when Dad sort of hinted that prison was also where one learned to play with oneself. (My mother, on the other hand, believed that was where you ended up after such behavior.) After that I never really believed them, because I knew I had never been to prison, and had never known anyone who had been either...." — *Minister*

"In 1976, when I was a senior in college, my parents both took me aside and said, 'If your friends ever find out that you're sleeping with your boyfriend, they won't have anything to do with you! Nobody wants to sully their reputation by associating with people like that!'
"I started to laugh, which was apparently the wrong thing to do. My mother started crying, my dad started blushing and then he stomped out of the room." — *Homemaker*

"My parents thought of shame as some sort of crowd control method on my sister and me. My sister thinks she's a highly moral person because she's still thoroughly ashamed of herself for everything she is and does.
"The only thing of value I've learned in my life is that shame is not the same as truth." — *Salesperson*

"We had a very businesslike, no-nonsense family. Once during college, I brought my clothes home to be washed, and my mother thought my underwear was ragged, so she went out and bought me all new underwear. Then she *billed* me for them.
"But the best part was that she said she did it because if I ever met some nice girl, I shouldn't be embarrassed by underwear.
"I was so grateful to her for not getting euphemistic on me and talking about car wrecks and what the doctors would think." — *Accountant*

Advice on How to Live Your Life:

"My father told me, 'Never say anything unless it improves on silence.' I left home the day after my high school graduation, and haven't stopped talking since. Anything and everything

improves on the sort of silence I grew up with."
— *Art director*

"When I was in school, my father told me, 'Unless you snap out of it, it won't matter what you do for a living, you won't do very well at it.' "
— *Sales representative*

"My uncle used to tell me, 'It's a good thing you're in politics, because you're too lazy to farm and too dumb to run your own store.' "
— *Political aide*

"I used to get endless lectures about taking responsibility, working hard and not being lazy. It just made me feel irresponsible and lazy, till I figured out that my parents were trying to get out of the same chores I was. They wanted *help*, not a perfect child."
— *Systems analyst*

"My mother's main advice was 'If something's worth doing, it's worth doing well.' But because she could do everything so much better than I could, I always wanted to tell her to do it herself so it *would* be done well, or at least done her way."
— *Beautician*

"The only advice my father ever gave me was:
1. Don't go into a curve too fast. You'll go off the road.
2. The road near a grove will be icier in winter.
3. Life will be easier if you never go to a girl's apartment by yourself.
I've always been careful to observe the first two rules."
— *Sales representative*

"My parents had the P.Y.E.O. rule. No matter what we did: 'Put that stick down — You'll Poke Your Eye Out! Get out of that tree — You'll Poke Your Eye Out! Don't go down by the lake — You'll Poke Your Eye Out!'

"But the one that always baffled me dealt with my Space Cadet helmet. It was a huge clear plastic globe. I had already bounced it down the stairs a couple of times just to see how tough it was, but when I put it on one afternoon, my mother

yelled out the kitchen window, 'Take that thing off! It'll Poke Your Eye Out!'"
— *Men's clothing salesman*

"Most of my dad's advice had to do with hunting: Squeeze the trigger, don't make any noise, sit still — stuff like that.

"None of it has been of any value whatsoever."
— *Pharmacist*

"My mother used to tell my brother and me whenever we went to a gas station restroom to turn on the water faucet full blast so the attendant wouldn't know why we went in there."
— *Shipping clerk*

Advice on How to Raise Your Kids:

"My mother-in-law walked up to me at a picnic the month after my first child was born, put on her traffic-cop voice and asked, 'Well, how's your milk production?'

"Everybody in the park turned around, and when I didn't say anything, she must have figured I had something to hide, so she told me (and everyone else within earshot), 'If you'd drink one dark beer a day, you'd have better milk production, and your baby will be less fretful!'"
— *Lawyer*

"My own mother used to tell me that the starving children of Africa would love to finish my green beans. I hated that line.

"But when my own son balked at mowing the grass one day, I pulled an updated Third World guilt trip on him and yelled, 'If you had been born in Nicaragua, you'd be in the army by now and *really* have to work!' He just looked at me as if I had suffered a nervous breakdown."
— *Writer*

"When I got married and had kids of my own, I had to work through a lot of my feelings for and towards my dad. Finally, I wrote him a letter telling him how much he did for me and how much he meant to me. I wanted to tell him that I loved him, but I also wanted to know whether he loved me.

"Then I dropped it in the mail and waited for some response. I guess I should have sent it as a registered letter so I would have known whether he ever received it, because he never mentioned it." — *Lawyer*

Unexpected Advice:
How to Let Them Know What They Did Wrong

"We had spent two years restoring a 200-year-old house in Pennsylvania to match the colonial original. At an informal housewarming party at the end of our work, one of the neighbors told us: 'You know, this house is really going to look nice once you get it all fixed up.'" — *Doctor*

"There was a farewell party at work, and one of the women in marketing just walked up to one of the women in accounting and asked, 'Do you find that you still like your hair style as much as what they're wearing nowadays?'" — *Corporate trainer*

"After college, I dated a woman who lived on the East Coast, and things had gotten serious enough to talk about marriage. One day I got a phone call from her:
" 'Hi,' she said. 'I'm getting married.'
" 'I know we are,' I answered.
" 'No,' she said, 'Not you. Just me.'
I have no idea what the rest of the conversation was about." — *Computer programmer*

" 'I love you so much for the things you are, but for the rest of it, I don't know what to do about you!' I had known this person for quite some time, but I still don't have any idea what they meant." — *Teacher*

"I used to wear white clogs to work all the time, till a colleague brought me a brand-new pair of shoes and said, 'Here! Now you don't have to wear those any more.'" — *Nurse*

"People give fathers advice they wouldn't dream of giving to a woman. They must not believe we can be good caretakers. A woman came up to me in the park one summer day and told me: 'Your baby only has on one sock. He's going to catch a cold!' I must have looked startled, because then she said, 'If he *does* get a cold, you can just stuff his shoes with mooshed up garlic and onions, and that should take care of it.'"   *—Photographer*

Quick Reminders:

1. Don't run through the lawn sprinklers. You'll get a sore throat (or catch polio).
2. If you eat grass, your stomach will explode.
3. Never put coins in your mouth. They're used to hold dead people's eyes shut.
4. If you eat too much jelly too quickly, you'll get stomach worms.
5. If you eat cookie dough (or hot bread), it will make a hard ball in your stomach and you'll die.
6. If you swallow gum, it will stick all your insides together, and you'll get terrible cramps (or starve to death).
7. If you swallow your gum, it will stay in your stomach for seven years.
8. Wade in mud puddles and you'll get the Mully Gubbles!
9. If you eat apple seeds, a tree will grow in your stomach and the branches will stick out of your ears.

MUSHROOM HUNTERS TURN DESPERATE

The Morel Appreciation League of Minnesota today demonstrated its latest attempts to foster growth of Minnesota's rarest delicacy, the morel mushroom.

"All scientific efforts at normal cultivation have proved ineffective," stated group leader DeWayne Aufderheide (right). "And we didn't get any help from crystals or channeling either, although my wife claims to have been in contact with a 9,000-year-old morel named Har-Rol."

"The only thing left was to take matters into our own hands," said Lavonne Nonnemacher (center). "We sort of dance around stumps and old logs, and sprinkle the ground with melted butter, to show the little morel seeds how much they're loved and how desperately we want them to succeed."

Claims Mrs. Delmer Schmadebeck (left), "We think the costumes make us sort of a role model and help us establish a mentor relationship with the little fellows."

Boiled Cabbage and Fried Sausage:

Cooking for the Troops

Kaiser Wilhelm tried to limit German women to *"Küche, Kirche, Kindern."* German/American women have spent quite some time crawling out from under that KKK, despite recent attempts by the religious right to reinstate it.

Not that anybody is opposed to cooking, church and children, so long as they aren't used as a ceiling or a cell. In particular, German/Americans are *definitely* not opposed to cooking.

Society might eventually crumble without churches, and society couldn't continue for more than a century without children, but society is absolutely going to hit the ceiling within three hours if dinner isn't ready. That's called setting priorities.

German/Americans like *solid* food. Food that makes the plate rattle when it hits. Food with heft. Food with corners. Food that makes you sorry you ever finished the whole thing.

We are what we eat, and we eat our heritage every day. We like sausage whether or not it's the wurst possible meal. Anything we can run to the ground we will grind up into a wurst.

Because it is so intimately connected with our heritage, we use food as a symbolic pledge of allegiance to our parents, who essentially say, "Prove you love me — clean up your plate!"

And as with everybody, food is a form of one-upsmanship for German/Americans. The winner is the person who can produce the most authentically German food, using ingredients generally unavailable in the United States.

So stock up with Alka-Seltzer and waddle through our little food fair. You've *got* to keep your energy up, you know!

The Potato Diet

A lot of disinformation has been disseminated lately about potatoes. Some persons say they're fattening, they're starchy, they're not sleek like snow pea pods. These same people consider sushi a major protein source. The world is divided into people who want to die unless they look like string beans and those who don't mind looking like a kohlrabi.

Cellulite comes from an old Latin word meaning "screen goddess" and derives from an even older Greek word, *celluloid*, which means "old black and white movies shown at 2 a.m. on cable." It is no coincidence that all the great film artists have been potato eaters. Marlene Dietrich ate potatoes throughout her professional career. Who can forget the scene in *Der Blaue Engel* in which Dietrich feeds Emil Jannings slivers of raw potato? Jannings' sense of academic superiority crumbles as he succumbs to her potato magnetism.

Frederick, King of Prussia, was given the title "The Great" when he ordered everybody to plant potatoes so they'd stop starving. I always thought you had to slay a dragon or something to be called "The Great." If he had commanded the peasants to plant pineapples and been able to make it work, *that* would be worth a Great.

Why You Should Go on a Potato Diet

1. Potatoes are good for you because they give you that heavy, slow feeling that reminds you for hours that you've already eaten. We German/Americans have a lot on our minds. It's easy to forget we've already eaten lunch and sit down to another meal.

2. Boiling potatoes is easy. You don't have to sit there with a stopwatch worrying about how your guests will react if the potatoes aren't *al dente*.

3. On a potato diet, you can get your special dietary needs met anywhere in the country, usually deep-fried, so you also get more than 150 percent of your USDA-approved daily adult requirements of cooking fat.

4. Now that steroids are frowned upon, athletes who need to gain bodily bulk quickly can binge on potatoes as a way to top their opponents.
5. Eating potato skins is one of the chief courting rituals in today's society. If you are a stranger to potatoes, you will have no luck at singles bars and will die a virgin.
6. Eating hot french fries while driving is an excellent way to develop hand-eye coordination and other motor skills. Dropping one in your lap tests your reflexes as well as the skill of oncoming motorists.
7. Potatoes provide an excellent foundation for a class system. The lazy and slovenly buy only Potato Buds, even for Thanksgiving. The person truly dedicated to his or her heritage will lovingly peel and mash the real thing, even when no one is around to offer compliments.
8. Potatoes are powerful tranquilizers. When your children have stressed you to the breaking point, make them peel potatoes. The room immediately will fall silent, and you will be sedated.
9. Potatoes can be a powerful communications tool. By cutting a pattern into a potato and inking it, you can print things. This would be particularly helpful if you wanted to foment revolution but were way too broke to print up pamphlets.
10. Potatoes are weapons. They can be thrown at cats, dogs and presumably even invading Russians, although the Russians might just eat them. Write to your congressional representative and demand the right to bear potatoes! When potatoes are outlawed, only outlaws will have potatoes!

Unavailable Ingredients:
The Secret of German Cooking

Like everything else in German/American life, cooking has a rating system so you can tell when you're doing it wrong. Because we German/Americans prefer to internalize our rules and prohibitions, there's no need for a system of written warnings. You *know* when you've sinned.

This system is matrilineal and is based on authenticity. Authenticity means doing whatever Great-Grandma Strehlau did. Never mind that Great-Grandma was a Bavarian peasant who cooked with flour that had the consistency of sawdust and who was thrilled to get a scrap of dried fruit for a treat. Only backpackers live like that nowadays.

German/American cooks wish they still lived like that. Then they would be doing things authentically, as Great-Grandma did. If Great-Grandma went to extraordinary lengths to get rare ingredients for her *Stollen*, then so must you today, or risk being unauthentic.

This is why German/American cooks make such a big scene every October at the grocery store about getting authentic candied Black Forest cherries. Only *lazy* cooks settle for the bargain cherries (that are probably smuggled in from Iran) at the discount store.

We all fall short of authenticity, just as we all fall short of God's grace. The difference is that God doesn't judge us as harshly as we judge ourselves. But little sinners that we are, we also know how to make authenticity work in our favor.

Example: At the big Christmas party, you serve your *Stollen* with a flourish. Your guests are slow in their praise, so you decide to whip them into line. As you force second helpings on them, modestly accept their faint praise and say, "Well, this isn't the way Great-Grandma Strehlau used to make it. . ."

Pause to let them focus on the seriousness of what you're about to say next. Then dump it on them: "You just can't get good angelica here!"

You've snatched victory from the jaws of defeat. You've

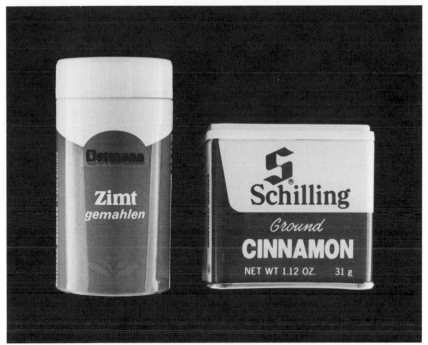

Which cinnamon is better? Was there ever a doubt?

proved that you are so authentic that you can tell the difference between American angelica and German angelica. The women will all be impressed, as will the men, despite the fact that none of the men know what angelica is.

You Can't Get It Here!

To thoroughly protect your rear while cooking, you must learn proper defensive culinary skills.

Know where to place the blame. Blaming your spouse for interrupting you for a little unscheduled romance will win you absolutely no sympathy unless he/she backed you into the stove.

The best bet is to blame your basic ingredients. German/Americans, like Germans, believe that the higher you go on the pyramid, the less guilt there is.

Some ingredients are available only in Germany. Some

ingredients haven't been available even in Germany since our ancestors left during the last century.

Some ingredients may *appear* to be available in the United States, but every good German/American cook knows that they're not quite as good as the German versions. There's just no way a cookie made with American cinnamon could be as tasty as a German cinnamon cookie.

Each of the ingredients listed below offers a ready excuse for a dish that could have tasted better. Just remember Anderson's #1 Cooking Rule:

> When in doubt, double the sugar.
> When in trouble, blame the ingredients.

Placing the Blame:
Ingredients as Scapegoats

Below are 25 ingredients that are perfect cooking scapegoats. Careless cooks might think that the American versions of these ingredients would be just as good as the German versions. That just shows how little they know about being authentic!

angelica	hundreds and thousands
aniseed	juniper berries
apricot jelly	mixed candied peel
cinnamon	mocha
chocolate	morello cherries
crystallized violet petals	nutmeg
desiccated coconut	plums
ginger	poppy seeds
gelatin, white	potato flour
gelatin, leaf	vanilla sugar in sachets
German butter	tinned chestnut puree
German sour cherries	wild berries from the German forests
German-style rye flour	

Food as Duty

A duty is something you do gladly to show respect. Respect is due to our parents, our teachers and our religious leaders. Food is a duty, but only one of the above categories regularly feeds us. Food, therefore, is a duty to our parents.

We show our respect to our parents by dutifully cleaning our plates. This also keeps all hell from breaking loose in the house and makes it more likely that we will get the Nintendo game we've been coveting.

While the following rules are so thoroughly understood by German/American children that they don't even need to be spoken aloud, those of you who have married into a German/American family could use some guidelines for understanding your spouse.

Check out your spouse — or yourself — for these little insights.

1. Food is your mother's way of proving that she loves you and is a nurturing parent, even when she has to scream at you to finish your meal.
2. It is your parents' job to feed you. While they do their job very well, even as a kid you know how adults really feel about their *jobs.*
3. Your job as a child is to show proper respect and enthusiasm for the meals your mother has cooked. Every day that you do this is another happy day for your mother, one more day that she doesn't think she was insane to quit a perfectly good job to stay home just to play Chutes and Ladders with a 4-year-old.
4. Respect is never uniform, and you are allowed the same picky eating habits as your father. You are not allowed to describe anything on the table in language that another 4-year-old would find hilarious. Remember your parents' advanced age and delicate sensibilities, and never say anything you wouldn't be embarrassed to say on "Mr. Rogers' Neighborhood."
5. When relatives come over for dinner, you must show them even more respect than you would your own parents, because they have probably forgotten that even 10-year-olds occasionally eat lemon meringue pie with their fingers.
6. Grandparents are due the most respect of all, because

they are the source of nearly all toys. While you may be proud of your developing language skills and sense of perception, you must *never* say that Chicken McNuggets look just like Grandma, all brown and wrinkled.

7. It is ethnically insensitive and historically inaccurate to eat long-strand spaghetti with your fingers by dropping it into your mouth and then describe the process as "eating spaghetti like the Indians." No Native American nation ever ate long-strand spaghetti in that manner. They nearly all preferred tortellini filled with pemmican in a white sauce.

8. Remember that you are a reflection on your parents at all times, and the spies that George Orwell wrote about really exist in school cafeterias. One misstep and your parents will hear about it. Two infractions and you'll never be taken to McDonald's again. Three offenses and you'll be put on a national list of people who are never in their life to be allowed into a restaurant with cloth napkins.

9. The difference between real restaurants and McDonald's is that restaurants for grown-ups do not have a drive-thru window. If, in a moment of weakness, your parents take you to a grown-up restaurant, they do not want to hear: 1. that you hate to get dressed up; 2. that the food looks funny; or 3. that there are no french fries. They know that. That's why they came here.

The Kraut-Pleaser

Ever since she was a little girl, Theresa Schwenges dreamed of opening her own restaurant, where she could make people eat what was good for them.

As a little girl, she turned her doll house into a doll restaurant. Instead of spanking her dolls when they were bad, she'd make them sit by the front door, where she'd tell them every few minutes, "There still aren't any tables in the no-smoking section. Would you care to sit between a pipe smoker and three

**Theresa, the Kraut-Queen, proudly displays
her new menus printed on VW hubcabs.**

people with cigars?"

She got in considerable trouble for "bucking the system" in high school when she did an extra-credit report criticizing the hot lunch program. While the principal was pleased with her call for more lunchroom monitors, "because no one can enjoy their meal when a small minority are misbehaving," he hit the ceiling when she brought to the school board's attention the special meals prepared for school administrators.

After high school, Theresa went to Vo-Tech to study nutrition and hospitality management, where she soon realized that the public didn't think that hospitality and nutrition had much in common. She also learned that her own ideas about hospitality were pretty much based on her grandmother's attitudes about food.

Grandma Pfau loved to cook. She loved to see people eating what she cooked. But if you didn't eat enough, or fast enough, Grandma would press a hot soup ladle onto the back of your hand, and you would wake up and eat a little faster.

It wasn't exactly compulsion, but in Grandma Pfau's kitchen, all the extra incentive to eat was in that soup ladle. Theresa was aware that she couldn't scold or scald her patrons into eating properly, but if Grandma didn't need ferns and antiques hanging from the walls to make hearty eaters, Theresa saw no reason to get involved with expensive and untried notions.

Her anti-fern sentiments were well known around campus, which made the trendier students nickname her "The Formica Fraulein." She caused quite a scandal when she criticized La Mandragola, a particularly chic new trattoria, by saying that the chef used too much garlic, and garlic was nothing but the ketchup of intellectuals.

Despite her conservative nature, Theresa was intrigued by New Wave nostalgia restaurants that served meat loaf at escargot prices.

In one class, "Theory and Trends in the Hospitality Industry," she learned that these places were called "Mom food" or "comfort food" restaurants. In Theresa's experience, "Mom," "comfort" and "food" were mutually exclusive notions.

"Comfort food" was the familiar, dull food that we all ate as children, transformed into a culinary security blanket to relieve the stresses of adult life. The idea of shaking down some big-city type for $9.95 for a lunch of Kraft Macaroni & Cheese was endlessly amusing to Theresa.

But the further she got away from Grandma Pfau's hot soup ladle, the more sense comfort food made to her. She thought about setting up a restaurant in her hometown specializing in German/American comfort food: Braunschweiger sandwiches on white bread with Miracle Whip and lettuce, mashed potatoes, lots of sausage and, of course, Jell-O.

The problem is that comfort food is nostalgic, and nostalgic means past tense. You can't be nostalgic about food you ate as recently as lunch, and you sure aren't going to get an old German/American farmer to shell out $9.95 for a plate of Kraft Macaroni & Cheese.

People in a small town go to a restaurant to get *away* from home cooking. They've had home cooking until their arteries are about to snap shut. "Home cooking" is a lot like "family values." It's a concept that everybody thinks refers to somebody else's home or family. Ward and June Cleaver's, maybe.

One of the big lessons of the 1950s that everybody missed is that simply being female, married and stuck at home doesn't make you a good cook. And we all know (and don't particularly want to talk about) the values of our own families. That's why good therapists are in such demand.

Theresa had worked herself into a dead end. Her teachers and friends from school weren't much help. When she explained that she wanted to open a German/American restaurant, her teacher suggested that she open a Chinese/German restaurant instead. (The drawback was that an hour after eating there, people would be hungry for power again.)

That was when Theresa's natural sense of exasperation gave her a crucial insight. Home on break, she went with her younger brother and his irritating friends to McDonald's. Watching them eat, she realized that kids don't much care what the food looks or tastes like, so long as they can eat it with their fingers.

Here were good German/American kids eating french fries at a restaurant with a Scottish name, run by a Swede from the next county! In a frenzy, Theresa scrawled out the concept for her new German fast-food restaurant.

Theresa's new restaurant would combine her heritage (which would please the older folks) with fast-food efficiency

FAST FAMILY DINING WITH AN OLD WORLD CHARM
NO SUBSTITUTIONS

A P P E T I Z E R S

Sauerkraut Soup **$1.95**
Beer Cheese & Crackers Soup **$2.25**

K R A U T   K O N T R O L

Sauerkraut Surprise **$3.95**
One huge sauerkraut ball hiding a different filling every week! A taste trick or treat!

"The In-Kraut" . . . . $~~3.75~~
Sauerkraut rolls fried in a spaetzle coating. Tangy and fun to eat!

Sauerkraut Supreme **$5.65**
*A whole platter of kraut, with boiled kartoffel klumps and bratwurst oozing oils
all over your chin. Feeds a family of 6.*

W U R S T   C H O I C E

Wurst Possible Case **$3.50**
A sausage explosion! 7 kinds of sausage on a pumpernickel bun with schnitlauch!

Personal Wurst **$2.75**
*Just enough to give yourself a little nurturing, plus just enough extra to feel
guilty about tomorrow!*

BLITZ FOOD

Heritage Burger . . . . $ 4.95
"The Works!" ½ lb. hamburger with horseradish, Limburger cheese & kraut.
Served on solid pumpernickel crusts!

Schnitzel on a Stick $3.75
Schnitzel with schnitlauch breading, over-fried just the way you like it!

Braunschweiger Balls $3.25
Bite-sized, breaded and deep-fried. You can't get better liverwurst!

Kartoffel Klumps $2.50
Deep-fried, boiled or mashed, they'll put some meat on your bones.

KINDER KRAUT

Brats von Nuggets $2.75
A whole basket of little bitty bite-sized brats, each one a mini-snack!

Sausage Wheels . . . . $2.50 ~~$3.25~~
Summer sausage slices on a pretzel stick axle. Enough for a little 4x4 appetite!
All that's missing are the sound effects!

Bitty Brats $2.00
Little tiny wieners for little tiny Kinder. Biodegradable, so it's no problem if they're
stuck up noses or in ears.

ON THE LIGHT SIDE

Turkey Schnitzel $4.75
If you didn't look, you'd swear you were eating Wienerschnitzel! Flavored,
breaded and overcooked just the way Americans like it.

Turkey Brats . . . . $ 2.40
No oils, no cholesterol! Just a day-long aftertaste to remind you of a great meal!

DESSERTS

Karmel Kraut $2.50
The ultimate in sweet & sour taste treats! You've never had anything this tart
stick to the roof of your mouth before!

Black Forest Torte $3.50
Reason enough to leave home and move to southern Germany!

Minnesota Valley Torte $1.75
Same as the Black Forest torte, except it's made by Sara Lee.

(which would please everybody else). It would serve traditional German food modified so it could be eaten standing up. Theresa would call her restaurant The Kraut-Pleaser.

Theresa leased the old Hoffmeier Farm Equipment building out on the highway. When word got out that Theresa had bought Charlie Kranz's old stuffed moose head at the auction, most of her mother's friends stopped by. They just wanted to see how the redecorating was coming. By the way, they had been going through the attic, and could she use another mounted set of antlers? Or a stuffed muskie? No, they wouldn't *dream* of taking money for it. God knows, their husbands had been killing and stuffing things all their married lives, and they'd long ago run out of nephews who would accept mounted deer horns as a Christmas present.

Theresa's friend Marie down at the Move-it! Travel Agency gave her a couple of nice travel posters from Germany, and Theresa found several wagon-wheel chandeliers, which went nicely with the knotty pine paneling and added the final touch.

When The Kraut-Pleaser opened, the local paper did a flattering feature on Theresa. What particularly impressed the reporter was how careful Theresa had been with her money. "Restaurant Almost Paid for by Time It Opens" read the headline.

In the years since then, Theresa has established herself as a shrewd businesswoman as well as someone dedicated to her heritage. The only change she's had to make came about four years ago, when she altered her sign out front from "Fast Food with an Old World Charm" to "Fast Family Dining with an Old World Charm." (She knew she was right in breaking up with her boyfriend from school when he suggested, in all earnestness, that she adopt the motto: "Eat Your Heritage.")

Theresa would like you to know that she'd be happy if you stopped by for dinner, but she's not going to beg or anything.

Wurst Possible Choice

Germans make fast automobiles because anything that *doesn't* move fast enough in Germany is in danger of getting ground up into sausage. There is even a *Touristenwurst*, although I don't believe it's anybody any of us knew.

Many German sausages were born of hard times, when every source of protein was considered fair game. But even famine-crazed people refused to touch certain items. The only way to get people to eat these things was to grind them up and smoke them.

Be realistic. How hungry would you have to be to chow down on a meal of solid pork fat, pork tongue and blood? But you probably grinned your way through a snack of *Blutzungenwurst* during your last trip to Germany. Chalked it up to cultural diversity and great foods of Western man. If you were smart, you probably didn't ask the English-speaking waiter what you were eating.

As someone who grew up on countless lunches of Braunschweiger on white bread (this is *America*, for heaven's sake), I'd like to give a quick listing of German sausages and, just to be mean, their ingredients. If you're still standing at the end of the list, you can reread Upton Sinclair's *The Jungle*, about the American hot dog industry.

Personal Wursts

Bierwurst — Solid pork fat, pork butts and lean beef. So named because the sausage is slow-cooked in beer, just like many of the people eating it.

Bratwurst — Fresh pork shoulders and lean pork trimmings, beef and spices. The Germans would really rather have you fry this. It's bad enough that Americans insist on barbecuing it, but they will not stand idly by while some idiot yuppie tries to mesquite-grill it. There *are* limits!

Blutzungenwurst — Diced, solid pork fat, pickled pork tongue, pork snouts, pork skins, beef blood and black pepper. You can about imagine how much pepper it takes to make this palatable. You wouldn't miss a whole lot if you steered clear of anything with the word *Blut* in the title.

Braunschweiger Leberwurst — Pork liver and pork jowls. Great with white bread, Miracle Whip, lettuce and cold milk, particularly if you are 8 years old and don't care that you're eating pork snouts and beef tripe.

Frankfurter Würstchen — Prime lean pork, ground to a fine paste and cold-smoked. Looks like Vienna sausages. Anything Germans can't describe they say, "Looks like Vienna sausages," just as Americans say every bizarre meat, from rattlesnake to guinea pig, "tastes just like chicken."

Hamburger gekochte Mettwurst — Coarse, lean pork. Hamburger has been referred to as "German sirloin," mostly by the French.

Mettwurst — Smoked pork, veal, pork trimmings, bull meat, pork back fat and boneless Boston butts (no jokes about Dukakis please). These short, stubby sausages are also known as *Teewurst* or *Schmierwurst*, which pretty well sums it up.

You can break the hearts of the people of Westphalia, Hamburg and Hanover just by saying you like the *Mettwurst* from Rugenwald better than theirs.

Pennsylvania Dutch Scrapple — All purpose pork meat (ears, snouts, jowls, etc.), beef cheeks or hearts, white corn meal and onion chips. And you thought we lost the knack for making irritating food when we immigrated to America!

Pinkelwurst — Groats, pork fat, pork and cereal. People who know what groats are consider this a delicacy when it's served with kale that has been cooked in lard.

Sülze (headcheese) — Coarsely sliced pieces from a hog's head and the gelatin from pigs' feet. It resembles "a fine aspic," if you believe that.

Schweinebauch mit Mohrrüben — Not strictly a wurst, but

anything that consists of pig's belly cooked with carrots and served with boiled potatoes in a light sauce would qualify for this list.

Thüringer Blutwurst — Extra-lean pork trimmings (or skinned fatted shoulders), pork cheeks, pork hearts, pork fat and blood. Good Thüringer should have a consistently sour flavor, for reasons I don't understand.

There is a semidry Thüringer that should be served with beer, because it is hard to imagine a semidry German.

Touristenwurst — Three-fourths beef, one-fourth pork, or so they say. It really *does* translate as "Tourist Sausage." I'd recommend that you just keep moving and stay off country roads at night.

Turkey or Chicken Wieners — Boneless chicken or turkey, chicken or turkey fat and ice water. Fake sausage for fake meals. Available only in America, it nicely compliments elbow macaroni and Jell-O.

Trüffel Leberwurst — Pork, pork liver and truffle. Only Germans would grind up a truffle for sausage.

Dry-Cured Westphalian Ham Sausage — Lean beef, lean pork, bacon and good rum. Perhaps the rum helps you forget that there isn't any ham in this ham sausage.

Weisswurst — Veal, brains and secret herbs. These tiny, delicately flavored, pale white sausages are sold only in Bavaria. They must be eaten within 12 hours, because they "deteriorate quickly." In other words, you can practically hear them ticking.

Wieners — Lean bull trimmings, beef cheeks, skinned pork jowls, trimmed pork cheeks, fat pork trimmings, fat beef trimmings, pork fat and pork butts.

Here is a wurst with a geography problem. Is it from Vienna (Wiener) or is it a good Frankfurter? In America, all hot dogs come from the baseball park, but the commissioner assures me that they have all tested negative for steroid use, even the foot-long ones.

A Quick Survey of the Wurst Ingredients:

All German Wurst is divided into four types, and there are at least 130 known varieties.

Whatever kind of wurst you get, you will be eating things that will be new and amazing to you. Here's a little list of the wonder ingredients that help German/American bodies grow in so many ways and in so many unexpected places

WURST STUFF:

Back fat
Beef flanks
Beef blood
Beef cheeks
Beef hearts
Beef navels
Beef plates
Beef tongue
Beef tripe
Beef trimmings
Beef trimmings, fat
Boneless Boston butts
Briskets
Lean bull meat
Very lean bull trimmings
Chuck
Cow meat
Lean cow meat
Very lean cow trimmings
Lean elk
Groats (whatever the heck they are)
Ham
Pork back fat
Pork butts
Pork butts, lean
Pork butts, boneless
Pork butts, lean boneless
Pork cheeks

Pork cheeks, trimmed
Pork ears
Pork fat
Pork hearts
Pork jowls
Pork jowls, skinned
Pork livers
Pork, lean
Pork, very lean
Pork shoulders, fresh
Pork shoulder trimmings
Pork skins
Pork snouts (If you have difficulty obtaining pork snouts, feel free to substitute pork butts. Either end will do, apparently.)
Pork tongues
Prague Powder #1
Regular pork trimmings
Lean pork trimmings
Extra-lean pork trimmings
Special lean pork trimmings
Fat pork trimmings
Veal
Venison

Herr Yuk

There are limits, there really are, on economy. I understand that during famines, you have to grind up tree bark to mix with flour to stretch your bread. But there are some animal parts that should be used only as fertilizer under the tomatoes.

German/Americans understand this better than Germans do. We understand the karma of the sacrificial carp. Virile and vigorous tomatoes thrive on the blood of one carp per plant, placed in the hole during planting ceremony. Bullheads can serve the same sort of sacramental function.

In fact, anything that the Germans call "little meats" are well suited for this purpose. Whenever a German resorts to coy euphemism, watch out. They're hiding something that shouldn't stay hidden. "Little meats" is a sneaky term for barn-yard body parts that would gag most people if they knew what they were eating.

Here are some actual recipes from the kitchen of the famous German/American cook, Mrs. Fredrick (Elma) Krausse. Personally, I wouldn't recommend trying any of them, and I refuse to be held responsible if you're foolish enough to mess with them.

BREADED BRAINS

Take 1 pound of calf, lamb, pork or beef brains. I have no idea where you'd get them. I don't want to know.

Put them in cold water and wash off all the blood and take off the fine membranes. Are you ready to quit yet?

After they are completely clean and dry, cut them length-wise, salt them and bread them. Then fry them in very hot lard. Don't even *think* that you can fool your guests into believing they are eating cauliflower crudités.

BRAINS WITH EGGS

Acquire and clean brains as above. Just keep me out of it.

Pour a little melted butter and chopped parsley into a bowl with the brains, and moosh everything up with a wooden spoon till it all looks sort of whitish.

Siegfried Zitelsberger
starts each sausage
season with new
friends and the same
old reliable
equipment.

Add enough beaten eggs. Salt and pepper the whole thing, and cook. Don't add too many eggs. You wouldn't want to turn your little brains and eggs brunch into a passé repast of scrambled eggs 'n' brains.

Resist the temptation to overcook. There's no way you're going to disguise this stuff, and you only get points towards your Gourmet Merit Badge when you can actually feel the texture of the meal.

SOUR LUNG SOUP

If you can get brains, you can get lungs. I still don't want to know about it. Just go get a beef lung yourself or send Igor after it.

Cook the lung (clean it first, for heaven's sake), together with an onion, a bay leaf and any soup greens you think might help. Cover it so it can't crawl out, and boil that sucker hard for 30 to 45 minutes.

Once it has shrunk so much that it feels like liver (another story altogether) when you give it a little poke, take the lung out and slice in into noodle-like strips, in hopes that you can fool some people into thinking they're eating some exotic pasta.

Make some béchamel (or any old white gravy that comes to mind). Mix it into some of the strained broth, and pour in enough vinegar. Remember, suddenly, what you're eating and add another couple slugs of vinegar. Or maybe take a couple of slugs of something else to help you forget what you're about to eat.

This delicacy is supposed to have a "distinctly piquant flavor," which shouldn't be hard to achieve if you just tell your guests what they're eating.

MOCK OYSTERS

Get another brain. Clean it with your fingernails. Getting to enjoy this a little, no?

Soak it in water so all the blood comes out. Remember, we already talked about this. Cook, then cool.

Get out all your serving shells (real or ceramic) and line

them up. Slice the cooked brain lengthwise and put it in the shells.

Artistically arrange little piles of bread crumbs and anchovy butter atop each neurological slice. Bake them, or just nuke 'em in the microwave.

Makes a fine appetizer for the sort of person who enjoys eating oysters anyway.

TONGUE

Rinse well and cook a big raw beef, calf, pork or lamb tongue in boiling salted water all morning, and maybe most of the afternoon if you can't get up your nerve to look.

To check whether the tongue is still soft, pierce the tip with a knife. If you poke the sides, the tongue loses too much juice. Even dead body parts have feelings, you know.

You can slice the big tongues into ¾-inch slices, and slice the little tongues once, lengthwise. Slather with horseradish.

Better yet, just slather your own tongue with horseradish. When you recover, you won't be able to recall your own name, let alone whether or not you just ate anything.

HASENPFEFFER

Kill Thumper and throw out everything except the back and legs. Skin, wash and wrap with salt pork.

Stick this into a pan with butter, onion, carrots, celery, peppercorns, allspice and bay leaves. Everything Thumper himself would have loved.

Roast for a half hour, basting frequently. Put the vegies and gravy through a strainer and the kids will never suspect a thing.

FRIED CARP

Fried carp is considered a delicacy in Austria. But then, the Austrians are so crazy they think they'll turn into Englishmen if they call their coins schillings.

You can buy live carp in fine stores in Austria and watch while they gut it. Or you can choose not to watch. They don't care.

Take it home, and salt it good. Let that soak in and see if it tastes any better, although you know you're just kidding yourself.

Fry it slowly, but fry it. Raw carp is not a delicacy anywhere. Carp is best eaten from September to February, when you are so hungry you'd even eat, well, a carp.

BOILED CARP

Same as before, except boil it for an hour or so. Breading the carp before boiling isn't recommended.

ROASTED CARP

Same as before, except you artistically arrange the pieces in a roasting pan. Spelling out rude words with carp parts is considered unspeakably vulgar.

JELLIED CARP

Same as boiled carp, except you use more sliced onions. Put it in a nice dish and pour unflavored gelatin over it. Stick it in the refrigerator, and with any luck, you'll forget to bring it out at dinnertime. Serve with smelt Jell-O.

CARP SOUP

Why bother?

OXTAIL SOUP

Boil an oxtail for an hour with some barley. Add vegetables, onions, tomatoes and garlic. Cook forever, or until the meat drops off the bone. (If you leave the bones in the soup while serving, just remember that "informed consent" is a medical, not a culinary term.)

Then throw everything out if you can't remember cleaning that oxtail very, *very* well beforehand.

TOSSED SAUERKRAUT AND SMOKED FISH SALAD

This is a good recipe for people who are on a diet, because they won't be tempted to eat too much. Place a pound of sauerkraut in a large, stylish bowl, and gaily toss it into the air, taking care to cover yourself with a raincoat. Then spend endless hours deboning some smoked fish till your hands smell just awful.

If you're having Scandinavians over for lunch, you can throw in some tuna because they won't know the difference. Dump everything into the sauerkraut, add some red peppers for visual relief, some olives to confuse things, and enough sugar to cut the taste.

Serve at room temperature so your guests will have to face up to the reality of what they're eating.

PINEAPPLE SAUERKRAUT

Drain and dry some sauerkraut. If you're so lazy you don't even make your own sauerkraut, you'll just have to worry about the acidity. That's your problem.

Boil the sauerkraut in unsweetened pineapple juice till the kraut absorbs the juice.

Hollow out a pineapple, and throw the diced pineapple into the sauerkraut. Cook a little bit. Drain. Stuff everything back into the pineapple.

Serve with something else. This isn't a main course. What's the matter with you? You should know better!

PUMPKIN SAUERKRAUT

If you think you're so fancy, why don't you just go ahead and try that last recipe with pumpkins. Or apples. Or kohlrabi, or gourds, or anything. You're so smart! You don't need my help! You just think that you can hollow out anything and your guests won't know! See if I care!

Editor's Note: At this point, our cooking expert, Mrs. Fredrick (Elma) Krausse, started throwing things and had to be helped to a chair, where she explained that her kids never write to her and after a while it just gets to her.

To all the Krausse kids: Please, please write to your mother. Soon!

An experienced polka musician will have so many metal souvenir pins on his Tyrolean hat that the hat will be able to receive and transmit radio signals normally inaudible to the human ear. When this happens, the pain can be excruciating for even the bravest man.

Polka:
Aerobics for the Elderly

T here are those who contend that Polka Night at the Gibbon Ballroom isn't an authentic polka event if you can't smell a little manure clinging to someone's shoes.

There are those who say the best polka to be found today is at the wedding dances at George's in New Ulm, most likely one of the Catholic weddings, particularly one that involves two farm families, each with at least a hundred cousins, aunts, uncles, nephews, nieces and an Oma to keep an eye on everything.

However, purists say that Pure Polka no longer exists because the bands are too American and the beer is too lite.

But polka will survive and prevail, because polka is the music of defiance for rural German/Americans. Seventy-five-year-olds defy bad backs and trick knees to dance as if they were eternal. Farmers defy doctor's orders and tease that ulcer with just one more brandy and 7-Up. And everybody is tacitly defying the people who are conspicuously absent.

Because not *everybody* polkas. The Town Germans — the shop owners who haven't closed up yet and the small bankers who hold the farm loans — spend Saturday night at the Municipal Golf Club, where they get dressed up in plastic grass skirts for Hawaiian Night in the middle of February.

That's kind of a shame, and it seems to me they're missing something. Going to polka every Saturday night is a whole lot cheaper than joining some snooty exercise club. And there's nothing better to keep your heart in shape than a little defiance!

Deciphering the Medical Talk Between Polkas

After a certain age, disease holds the same sort of lurid fascination for us that sex holds for the young. We love to talk about both topics because talking relieves our anxieties.

Among German/Americans, this therapy takes place at two primary locations: at polka ballrooms, as an intermission between polkas; and in church basements, over the Jell-O and hot dish. Ballrooms and basements are where German/Americans go for a little mutual support.

German/Americans have a unique attitude about illness: It costs too much. Medical people say they can tell most people are beginning to feel better after a terrible operation when they ask for a mirror and a brush to do their hair. German/Americans are on the road to recovery when they start grousing about how doctors are overpaid and how little Medicare really covers.

The Techno-Teuton deep inside them keeps German/Americans from believing too deeply in miracles or the laying on of hands. When they get sick, they *do* want to know that you've been praying for them, but mostly so they can keep track of what you've been up to recently.

Notes From the Whoopee John Medical Symposium:

WHAT THEY SAY:
"She didn't come tonight, you know, because she's got that terrible awful stomach problem and she just feels pretty bad."
WHAT THEY MEAN:
"She's got terminal heartburn again because she eats like Purina was her cook."

WHAT THEY SAY:
"You know, that's going around! I had something like that last month, and the doctor said he had never seen a worse case..."
WHAT THEY MEAN:
"I was sicker than you!"

WHAT THEY SAY:
"He hasn't got out much since his hip started acting up again..."
WHAT THEY MEAN:
"He's going through his second childhood since he got that TV cable with the Playboy Channel."

WHAT THEY SAY:
"Oh, he's not doing so well. He's got the lumbago, the catarrh, bursitis and who knows what else."
WHAT THEY MEAN:
"That old hypochondriac! He's too lazy to even think up new diseases. His father used to complain about the same things, and nobody knew what he meant either."

WHAT THEY SAY:
"That sort of thing runs in their family, don't you know."
WHAT THEY MEAN:
(This phrase is only used to refer to bad backs, hay fever or the like. Such references as alcoholism or depression are never mentioned in public.)

WHAT THEY SAY:
"Ja, I got that flu that was going around, and that was just the hex!"
WHAT THEY MEAN:
"At my age, surviving three days of constant retching is a heroic achievement, and I want some congratulations!"

WHAT THEY SAY:
"Well, I went to see her in the hospital, and all she did was complain about how foolish it was to spend so much money for flowers and how terrible they charge for hospital rooms now!"
WHAT THEY MEAN:
"She's just as healthy and even tighter than her mother, and she lived to be 94!"

WHAT THEY SAY:
"Well, I went to see her in the hospital, and she said the nurses were so nice to her and the flowers were so pretty."
WHAT THEY MEAN:
"She's acting like one clean blouse is about all she'll need."

WHAT THEY SAY:
"His kids don't visit much anymore. He never did get along with any of them."
WHAT THEY MEAN:
"Considering how violent and abusive he was, it's amazing that any of them ever stops by."
WHAT THEY SAY:
"He needs to cut down a bit."
WHAT THEY MEAN:
"If he doesn't get into treatment, I'd give him about a year."
WHAT THEY SAY:
"He's got this new treatment for his arthritis that's got something to do with crystals..."
WHAT THEY MEAN:
"Don't forget that his father went bankrupt going to that arthritis clinic in Tijuana in the '50s too."

Aerobics:
Polka for the New Age

Aerobics is nothing but New Age polka that doesn't quite make it. The New Age is supposed to be nonauthoritarian, but aerobics classes are always led by some tyrannical anorexic who tolerates no physical dissent.

They are called classes to make you think you are going to get some profound insight from an expert. But unless you think that learning how *loudly* your heart can beat is profound, you might as well just sit down and listen to a rock, or a crystal, or something.

Aerobics can be either high-impact or low-impact, depending on the malice of your instructor. Polka only comes in a high-impact format and nobody needs any damned instructor to tell them what to do.

Both polka and aerobics involve a lot of free-form bouncing around, but it's more noticeable in aerobics because of the leotards.

Polka

I believe that if we weigh the strengths and weaknesses of each, we will find that polka is by far the better exercise.

Polka Positives

1. **BEER** — Nobody at the Bel-Rae Ballroom will get hysterical and scream about weight gain if you have a glass of beer during the actual polka exercise period.
2. **GOSSIP** — Polka people always know a lot of gossip. If they look around before they start talking, they're gossiping about someone at the dance. If they just start talking, they're gossiping about the town banker.
3. **NO LEOTARDS** — Polka people have nothing against tight clothes — just look at the shirts stretched across the better beer bellies. They just don't feel comfortable being seen in public wearing colors like ultra-violet raspberry, Day-Glo yellow or irradiated cobalt blue.
4. **NO SMUGNESS** — Polka people know they're just there for the beer, the gossip and a couple of good times around the floor. There's no sincere talk about empowering yourself to create an affirmative personal space for exercise.
5. **NO BACKTALK** — If you choose polka, nobody will lecture you about cholesterol, set points, maximum age-based heart rate, percentage of body fat or complex carbohydrates. You will not have to do stretching exercises beforehand, nor will you be quizzed on the major muscle groups.
6. **NO COMPULSIVENESS** — Some people see life as a marathon and think that it's time to get into serious training.

    By contrast, polka folks reason that if life really *is* a marathon, it's time to start some serious carbo-loading. Starting with the spaghetti dinner at St. Mary's parish tomorrow night.
7. **SPORTS CARS** — You don't see a lot of Porsches outside George's Ballroom when the Jolly Lumberjacks are playing. Polka people see no sense spending that

much money just to impress the sort of teenager who steals cars for a hobby. On the other hand, there aren't many Chevy pickups with Jazzercise bumper stickers either.

8. **SINGLES** — Polka dances are a good place to meet *nice* ladies. Not the sort who run around in swimsuits and purple long johns in the middle of the winter, but women who can cook and save money, and would make a good wife. Just the sort of woman both your mother and Father Tauscheck think you *ought* to be seeing.

Aerobics Affirmatives

This is a fair comparison. I'm willing to give aerobics its due, although I have deadlines to meet and cannot sit around all day trying to think of something nice to say. Lord knows, I've tried, and this is all I can come up with.

1. **LESS SMOKE IN ROOM** — The air is not filled with nicotine by-products. It is healthy, smoke-free air, filled only with sweat and whatever germs, viruses and pesticide-free garlic your fellow athletes have exhaled.

2. **NON-CONTACT LECHERY** — In a room full of heavy-breathing people dressed only in spray-on clothing, tawdry sexual fantasies are safe and easy, assuming that you aren't about to have a heart attack from overexertion. Simultaneously exercising and sucking in your stomach is a major cause of yuppie collapse.

3. **MIRRORS** — Most aerobics rooms have four walls of mirrors, so you can keep an eye on the one you truly love — yourself — while you sweat stylishly. The mirrors add the soft-porn feel commonly found only in those tacky honeymoon hotels that feature heart-shaped tubs.

A Little Polka for the Bride

Wedding polka dances are an ancient Bavarian form of birth control. Since custom demands that the bride and the groom both dance with everyone present, the young couple is so pooped by the end of the evening that they spend their honeymoon sound asleep. As soon as they wake up, the chivarees start. In a very traditional family, the parties can go on so long that some children don't get born for years.

The last big round of weddings I went to was when my friends all got married in a breeding frenzy after graduation. I don't know whether the same traditions still hold, since my friends' children aren't old enough yet to get married.

Weddings used to be full of symbolism and funkiness. The bride would be delivered to the cathedral in a manure spreader. Cleaned up, of course, but the symbolism was there: Be fertile. And wash once in a while too.

After the ceremony, the couple would be picked up at church and driven back to the farm in a wagon, just the two of them. Well, just the two of them and the polka orchestra. They'd polka all the way home, just in case they weren't already hyper enough. Nowadays, I suppose, the young couple just hop in the Honda and tune into an easy-listening station, but that's not the same.

Weddings seemed to go on for days, big jolly affairs, sort of like funerals, except there seldom were dances at funerals. You might think it would be easy to tell funerals apart from weddings. "That's easy — somebody's horizontal at a funeral!" would be the sort of smart remark a newcomer would make.

That doesn't take into account rental clothing and nerves. At the most solemn part of the marriage ceremony, just as the "I do's" came due, *somebody* would pass out, stone cold.

Grooms always have been the worst, because men lie about their size. Women have always known that men exaggerate some dimensions, but the real problem is *minimizing*. The groom goes down to rent a tuxedo and asks for a size 15½ shirt, knowing full well his neck zoomed past 15½ in 11th grade. But he thinks he can stand a tight collar for half an hour or so. Unfortunately, a wedding with a High Mass lasts at *least* an hour.

So there you have a 16½ -inch neck in a 15½-inch tourniquet and a groom getting glassy-eyed. All it takes is that little squirt in the blood pressure when it's his turn to say, "I do," and he's history.

Women aren't exempt. They have the same sort of fudge factor about waistlines that men have about necks. The difference is that men can rip off their bow ties as soon as they walk down the aisle, but a bride stepping out of her dress in the receiving line would cause quite a stir.

So brides pass out too. As do maids of honor, best men, mothers and, on at least one occasion, a flower girl. Fainting in weddings has always struck me as a political act, a nonviolent protest of the match, no matter what the medical experts say.

At least, that's how I remember my friends' weddings. Their first weddings, that is. Their second weddings have tended to be held in judges' chambers. Understated. Hoping they could slip into marital bliss without waking up the guard dogs.

But by and large, even weddings for the young now are saner than they used to be. We're discarding a lot of old rules that never did make much sense, like the bit about the groom not being able to see the bride before the ceremony. It just seems that if the bride is more than two months pregnant, you might as well waive that rule.

Like all rituals, weddings bring out the best and the worst in people and tell us more than we care to know about ourselves. If you're going to put yourself through the whole wedding thing, why not do it with the "Beer Barrel Polka" blaring in the background?

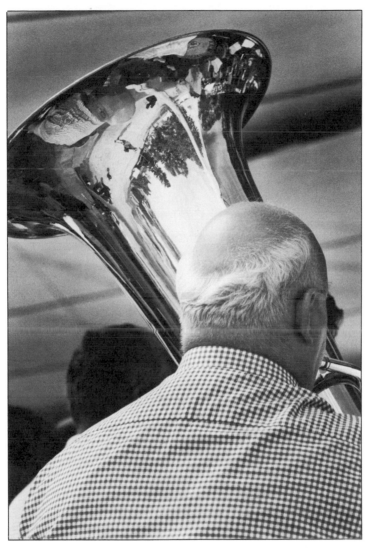

Polka is bulky music, played by bulky people, on bulky instruments, for dancers who see no reason to let *their* bulk get in the way of a good twirl around the dance floor.

The tuba player is a powerful man in German/American society, for it is he who puts the "Umph" in the Um-pa-pa. This doesn't exactly make him a Godfather, but you wouldn't want to alienate him just before your wedding dance.

A Polka Lexicon

Polka has its own language devoted to keeping *auslanders* on the outside. Like a lot of the *Platdeutsch* spoken in the United States, polka jargon plays fast and loose with the King's English and deliberately uses words in a rearranged fashion. For example: People who play polkas form an *orchestra*, not a *band*. Orchestras are respectable. A band is just a group of young punks with electric guitars and not a pot to pee in.

Here's how to sound street smart at a street dance.

ORCHESTRA — a 10-man musical group with brass, tubas and accordions, devoted to polkas, schottishes, ländler, etc.

BALLROOM — A place where you can polka. A "dance hall" is a word used only in 1950s westerns.

MUSIC — Polka. Beethoven. Bach. Mozart. Wagner. Strauss.

OLD TIME MUSIC — Polka. The good stuff.

JUNK — Everything else.

MODERN JUNK — Particularly bad everything else.

BRANDY — A warming fluid, mixed with beer or 7-Up, which helps produce *Gemütlichkeit*.

GEMÜTLICHKEIT — A German word meaning "the state of being happily potted" or "drunk, but not trying to punch anybody."

SOUSAPHONE — The tuba. The big one that looks like it ought to go on a diet.

LEDERHOSEN **AND TYROLEAN HATS** — What the authentically costumed polka orchestra wears. You will get in *big* trouble if you ask them where they got their Pinocchio clothes.

The Most Frequently Asked Question About Polka

"Why do the musicians always look catatonic?"
— *Puzzled, Boston, MA*

We're glad you asked that question, Puzzled. They're not catatonic. They're not even comatose or particularly short of breath. Polka musicians *always* look morose and disembodied because polka is an out-of-body experience for the performers.

These German/American Zen Masters go into trances when they perform, and their spirits leave the body to wander the universe. On a Saturday night, you can always see a crowd of astral polka bodies down at the tap room at Schell's Brewery. They leave their bodies at the dance to perform. Luckily, they've played the same songs so often, their central nervous systems can shut down entirely, and their arms and cheeks will keep on playing.

Unfortunately, when the central nervous system goes into cold shutdown, it takes the facial expression muscles with it. This is why polka musicians almost never smile and seldom swing and sway in their chairs. If you see a tuba player swaying, rush up on stage and catch him before he falls over. Those sousaphones could hurt a guy!

THE D.D.P.:
Economy in Government

One of FDR's most economical works projects, the D.D.P. (the Deutsch Ditching Project, or as Roosevelt's detractors dubbed it, the Dutch Ditcher Payoff) was instituted in 1939 and was responsible for the greatest expansion of wetlands drainage in America's history.

After consulting with local agricultural experts to determine need, the D.D.P. would gather 50 to 100 old German farmers with shovels. Precisely at 7:30 a.m., and in full view of these old Germans, the D.D.P. administrator would drop a dime down a gopher hole.

The resulting ditches reflect a Teutonic directness and thoroughness. The entire program cost the taxpayers only $321.40 for more than 216,000 miles of drainage ditches.

"Don't Throw That Away!":
Economy at Any Length

G erman/Americans believe in the saving ethic. This is not because we are compulsive pack rats, or even because we are the most retentive people on God's green earth. We save things so we can suffer.

At least we don't throw things out until we have suffered enough. Example: If you bought a towel 12 years ago for $11, the lazy person might think that you had, by now, gotten $11 worth of baths out of that poor, frayed old towel.

Not German/Americans. They haven't gotten $11 worth of *suffering* out of that towel. A towel ages, frays, gets holes and ceases to be useful. You get irritated every time you pick it up instead of a new towel. Now you've begun to suffer because of that towel, and you will feel cheated if you throw out that towel before you have wrung $11 worth of suffering from it.

This is *serious* economy. I mean, we're talking about double dividends at the Karma Savings & Loan, bookkeeper by appointment to St. Peter. Why do the very aged look so sad in nursing homes? They're worried that St. Peter will ask them about refrigerators that *could* have been fixed, skirts that *could* have been hemmed, and all the disposable kitchen napkins that were wasted in their lifetimes. They've been absolved of their other sins, and this is the only thing left hanging over their heads.

There is a darker side of our savings ethic. Perhaps we should start a Savers Anonymous therapy group, where we could overcome our instinct to squirrel away old light switches and fix antique lawn mowers under the pretense that we need a mower at the cabin.

The Dark Secrets of the Saving Ethic

Everybody jokes about garage sales but nobody talks about why the laughter is so nervous. Garage sales represent the death of the saving ethic, which was the only thing that helped Uncle August make it through the Great Depression.

If he hadn't saved that coffee can of bolts and screws, he would have gone broke taking his tractor into the dealership for repairs. Never mind that you're a computer programmer. You've saved every screw from every window latch you've ever changed. Someday you might *need* a totally rusty, one-inch screw with the screwdriver grip chewed off.

We wear our achievements lightly. We don't go down to the health club and casually drop hints about how many bolts we've saved, nor do we determine a person's status by how many tomato stakes they save from year to year.

But if your wife suggests throwing away something so vital as a box of used screen-door latches, or the hutch top for the dresser that was thrown out after the flood, you react from the heart. What would she know about saving things? A city girl, growing up in a suburb where the only thing they saved was corsages from charity balls! Throw out perfectly good stuff like that? Next stop, the poor farm!

At least that's the self-serving answer we give when we don't want to clean the house. The real reason is darker and less admirable. There isn't a jury in the country that would convict a woman who clubbed a husband who refused to throw out an old coat because it reminded him of his first girlfriend.

Let's look at some of the *real* reasons, the ones we can't admit out loud, for holding onto things:

The Dark, Secret Reasons for Saving Things

1. You can't throw out that letter jacket because I was wearing it the night I lost my virginity.
2. If I throw this out, it will set in motion a cleaning frenzy that will leave this house as empty as a monk's cell.
3. I don't care if it does smell like deer guts and mold, my dad gave me that old army cot. If I throw it out, he'll come back from his happy hunting grounds to haunt me.
4. That work bench came from my grandfather's house. He made it, and when I was a kid, he'd sit me on it, give me a sip of beer and tell me nasty gossip.
5. That teddy bear came from my high school sweetie who taught me how to give hickeys.
6. That Champagne bottle came from the party all us girls had before we got married. We got really drunk, and your old girlfriends, Cindy and Beth, told me *everything* about you, even how you go "Ohya,ohya,ohya,ohya,ohya" during sex, and we all laughed ourselves sick.
7. Don't throw away those notebooks. When I'm famous, they'll need those papers for my presidential library.
8. I'm going to rewire that toaster again! This time, I won't use wire that melts when you turn the heat on.
9. Those tapes are valuable! My big sister still thinks I tape-recorded her and her scudzy boyfriend necking in the rec room.
10. Throwing out this crepe pan would be admitting I'll never be as good a cook as my mother, and she'll make snide comments about how *she* never needed a career outside the home to be fulfilled.
11. Working on cars bores me now, but if I sell this tool chest at a garage sale, Bill will stop by and accuse me of being too good for the old gang.
12. If I throw out these old trophies, my grandkids will never believe I used to be such a hotshot jock.

14 Gift-Wrapped Night Gowns:
Closing Up Grandma's House

Alma Pelzl was as German as you could get. Frugal and careful, she mastered her every word, thought and deed. Because it was the economical thing to do, she grew tomatoes and zucchini (which she hated) and canned them for the winter, even after her doctor warned her against the kitchen heat during canning.

Her husband, the late William Pelzl, had done well in his business. Both Alma and William had always distrusted mass movements, sudden movements and sudden changes, so their home looked like an extremely accurate historical re-creation, a place where the air was still and the light was dark brown.

If the home was a time-warp, that suited William and Alma just fine. They wanted only the tried and true, the tested and the proven. They went on vacations, but when they came home, they never told anybody about their trips, and none of their friends ever thought to ask. Occasionally, Alma would bring back a tiny souvenir, but only if they had been to a place several times, or if she felt that the place was particularly prestigious, like southern Florida or Banff.

Their children grew up in that well-ordered house without breaking anything, unless you count the old clock, which their oldest boy Harold fixed once. Promptly at 3 o'clock, p.m. or a.m., it chimed 28 times. William finally decided that the clock was too old to stand the strain the mainspring put on it when it was wound, and it never ran again.

William passed on in 1969, shortly after he had bagged his first moose. His friend Charlie Huelskamp used to go around town telling everybody that the thrill of the shoot was too much for old Bill. Whether it was the thrill of the shot or the strain of dragging a 1,300-pound carcass, it did William in, and his widow donated the moose's head to the American Legion post to be stuffed in his honor, with a plaque below it which read: "Shot & Donated by M.Sgt. William D. Pelzl (Ret.) 1st Inf. Div., Company A, Bat. C, Participant, Argonne Offensive."

Alma wasn't certain about the Argonne Offensive, but the third line of engraving didn't cost any more, and it was a shame to pay for it and not use it.

Alma died in church, which undoubtedly pleased her. She was telling the minister that the missionaries in Central America were way too involved with politics and not enough with the gospel, and she just keeled over. Didn't say another word. Went to heaven denouncing liberals, and with her teeth set.

Her funeral was such a grand affair her friends couldn't help thinking she must have planned it before she passed on. There were big floral tributes from Eastern Star, the Women's Hospital Auxiliary, the Library Guild and the women's auxiliaries of both the American Legion *and* the V.F.W. The D.A.R. sent a nice note saying it was still investigating her admission request and asking whether it should continue, in case any of her daughters might want to join.

None of her daughters did. Having grown up in a home that looked and felt "like the inside of a piece of chocolate cake," as Ardis once put it, they had all moved out and away as quickly as possible.

All three of them had houses that were more windows than walls, according to Alma. The first time she visited Ardis's new house, she discovered to her horror that there weren't even shades in the bedroom. Alma slept in her bathrobe that night.

Maurine's home was even worse — one of those chrome and glass things that make you think you've been invited to J. C. Penney's for dinner. Alma never mentioned this to her children, for despite what they thought, she really did keep her opinions to herself a lot of the time.

The week after the funeral, Maurine, Ardis and their brother, Harold, got together to close up Alma's house. They were to be assisted by Maurine's oldest, Ann, and her husband, Jack, who had only recently married into the Pelzl family, and had to be dragged into helping.

Jack had his reasons. His family had once been friendly enough, but had split forever when his grandmother had died, and his aunts Charlene and Doris had started a fight over a gravy boat. Charlene said that Momma had always wanted her to have the china, and Doris had yelled that Charlene had stolen the china and made Momma's last years miserable looking for it.

Their brother tried to step in, but they both turned on him and let him know what they thought of his condescending ways. It was obviously a speech they both had intended to give for some time, because the performance was well-rehearsed.

The rest of the afternoon had turned into the sort of looting normally associated with civil disturbances, with three sets of sullen relatives carrying useless trivia to their car trunks. They didn't necessarily want it, but they had ahold of it, and they hated to give it up. By the time they were finished, there wasn't enough left for a garage sale, which was fine, because they would have fought about the proceeds from that too.

Jack was expecting a similar battle, and he hated to see it come before he got to know everybody in the family. Ann and Jack were the last to arrive, and found everybody standing around the living room table, reading obituaries, letters and notes from the funeral. Ardis had just picked up the D.A.R. letter and was about to say something typically Ardis when Maurine came in the room carrying a wooden box.

From the look on her face, it was important, and Jack started looking around for exits. "It's Momma's silver," Maurine announced with pride, as if she had just laid it herself. Jack was beginning to sweat. His wife stood between him and the door.

Maurine plunked the box down on the pile of letters to command everybody's attention and pried it open. Inside were 10 blackened place settings. None of the girls could remember their mother tolerating tarnished silver, and even Harold understood the implication.

No one had realized how poorly Alma must have felt. If Alma had been a hypochondriac, this would have been her revenge: "See! I really *was* sick!" It made them feel like bad children who had neglected their own dear mother in her last trials.

Maurine took the lead, as she enjoyed doing. She was the family historian and treasurer: "Momma got a lot of this silver at her wedding, and the rest she had to wait till the '50s to buy." Jack was fully ready for the fight now. Not only did this item have sentimental value, it represented some serious money. An outsider would pay cold cash for this, which is more than you could say about his grandmother's souvenir spoons, which his father and aunt were still feuding about.

It was like the first bell at a prize fight. Jack's adrenalin was flowing, despite himself, and he thought of saying something provocative just to get the ball rolling. Maurine and Ardis should be circling each other right now, looking for a jab or feint. HBO should be here to televise this!

And then it happened. Maurine drew herself up to her full height, turned to Ardis and asked, "Isn't this your pattern?" Ardis nodded as if she weren't paying attention, and Maurine pushed the silver chest over to Ardis.

That was it. No guttural mutterings, no innuendoes, no bargaining. What was the problem with these people? Didn't they love each other? Jack's family could shout in such a way that no one could accuse them of raising their voice. It was a skill, and it required lots of practice. And they got it, every time they saw each other.

By the time Jack came to his senses, everybody had disappeared. His wife was on her second trip carrying boxes into the dining room, and was giving him dirty looks. They loaded the table with boxes and set about sorting things into piles. Harold, Maurine and Ardis each had their own piles, as did Ann and Jack, but nearly everything went into the garage sale pile.

Someone would hold up an item, and if nobody spoke up, it went into the garage sale pile. Ardis and Maurine both spoke up for a box of sheet music from the 1920s, and Jack thought the blow-up finally had arrived. But Maurine just shrugged and said she couldn't play it on her electric organ, so Ardis might as well take it.

Jack had never realized how much hard work closing up someone's house could be. It's hard to feel tired when you're hysterical, and his family was always hysterical in these situations. Sort of like cleaning out the basement and having to carry everything through a minefield. At a time like that, you've got better things on your mind than sore shoulders.

Once Alma's shades were taken down and the sunlight came in full force for the first time in decades, things lost a little of their patina. Harold took a box of sea shells for his daughter who taught second grade, although no one could remember where they came from. In the yellow shade of Alma's rooms, things were cherished and understood. But she had forgotten to tell anyone about the connections, and today, her kids didn't particularly care. They had their own boxes of shells that they would never bother to explain.

When Ann let out a hoot from the bedroom, they all trouped up, desperate for a diversion. Ann was kneeling in front of the dresser, tidy boxes on all sides. The bottom two drawers were pulled out, revealing an array of department store boxes. A few of them still had ribbon around them, and some had both the ribbon and the wrapping paper, neatly folded and tucked under the ribbon.

Ann was reading aloud from a birthday card. It was a psychedelic card (as filtered through Hallmark artists) dated 1968. Ann had sent the card when she was 15, and had picked and paid for the nightgown herself. It was a granny-style dress, with calico flannel and lots of cream lace, a Lawrence Welk version of pioneer fashion.

The rest of the nightgowns weren't as easily dated, but everyone recognized at least one Christmas gift he or she had given their mother. Style wasn't a factor. There were warm nighties and slinky nighties, dull nighties and racy nighties (at least they were racy for a woman who regularly threatened to cancel her subscription to *Reader's Digest*).

There were 14 boxed nighties in all. Never worn, probably never even tried on. Still in their original boxes. Tidy. Waiting.

But what on earth for? Nobody could figure out why Alma was saving 14 nightgowns. Harold thought maybe she expected them to bury her in all 14, and Ardis said that considering how Alma felt about "that sort of thing," it was a surprise that she didn't wear two or three at a time so she wouldn't be so naked underneath her clothes.

Maurine and Ardis both took a couple of the nighties, but only after Harold practically threatened them. Those were old-woman nighties, and Maurine and Ardis were definitely not old women. Harold took the rest for his own wife, and his sisters wished they could be there to hear what she said when he gave them to her.

It turned out to be the emotional highlight of the day. Ardis and Maurine were right. They were old-woman nighties, and that's probably why Alma refused to wear them. They took theirs home and hid them in the bottom drawers of remote upstairs dressers. They felt old enough with their mother's death, and they didn't want to turn into her by putting on her nightgowns. Not just yet.

Real Family Heirlooms

Get rid of the glorious idea of donating all your belongings to a museum. The only museums that are interested in your German/American family heirlooms are ethnographic or historical museums, not high art museums. Instead of ending up behind a glass case, lovingly spotlighted, with your name on a tasteful little card, the heirlooms you donate will probably be used in a Touch 'n' Poke Program for second graders titled: "In Olden Days When Life Was Awful."

Let's be realistic. Most of our ancestors were draft-dodging, atheistic, utopian troublemakers. But they were shrewd people who realized that they had just about exhausted the limited patience of the authorities. So they left Mother Germany, one step ahead of some lawmaking body.

In those circumstances, we can be forgiven for leaving behind any *objets d'art* that might have accrued. It's not like Great-Grosspapa was the Count of Zipferstück and had to make the painful decision whether to take the silver reliquary or the gold and ivory table settings.

We brought mostly perishable heirlooms. Utopian tracts that a daughter either burned or gave to the county museum

Although no one can remember why, the Strehlau family continues to venerate this object because it is an heirloom.

when she got religion. A painted wooden bowl with a date and a name nobody recognizes. A stony refusal to recount our past lives. Not much to go on to explain the family to future generations.

Our ancestors didn't think something was an heirloom unless it was related to a triumph. They should have saved some of the heirlooms that related to their struggles. There were more of them than there were triumphs.

This is the sort of thing we should have been saving:

1. Great-Grosspapa's arrest warrant for participating in the student riots of 1848.
2. Great-Grossmama's club for protecting herself from thieves on the way back from selling her lace in Vienna.
3. Grossmama's only cookbook, *Deiner Freund, Die Kartoffel* (Your Friend, the Potato), containing 1,001 meals you could make from potatoes when nothing else was available.
4. The 1917 newspaper article calling Grandpa a "dirty Hun" for taking part in an antiwar protest.
5. The 1971 newspaper article calling you a "dirty Commie" for taking part in an antiwar protest.
6. Great-Grosspapa's deed to his farm from the U.S. Government, with land listed at 25 cents per acre.
7. The 1920 deed to Grandpa's farm, when land cost $69.31 an acre and a tractor cost $750.
8. The 1940 deed to your father's farm for $1,312, which he was able to pay off in three years.
9. The 30-year mortgage to your farm, the loan on your $68,000 tractor and any other correspondence you may have had with your bank recently.
10. Examples of a wishful-thinking collection. Include Grandpa's goat gland and arthritis clinic cure in Juarez, Mexico; your mother's Laetrile receipts; your Jerusalem artichoke investment plan; and your daughter's book, *Crystals Can Cure AIDS!*
11. Your parents' *bad* report cards. Haven't you ever wondered why your mother has every report card she was ever issued, except for the third grade?

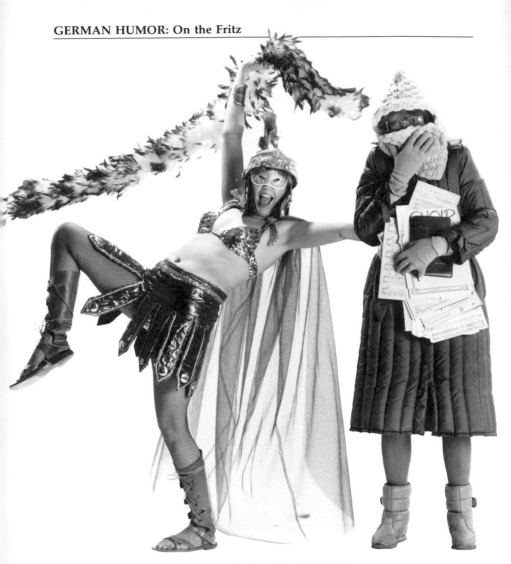

REACTIONS TO FEBRUARY
DIFFER ACCORDING TO RELIGION,
SCIENTISTS DISCOVER

Catholics and Lutherans react differently to February. Catholics like to kick up their heels and go to Mardi Gras. Lutherans know that if you kick up your heels, you'll lose your footing on the ice.

If Lutherans ran Mardi Gras, we'd all prepare for Lent by going to choir practice, not by running around half naked in the streets looking like a Roman Legionette.

The Slow Grinding of Teutonic Plates:

Catholics and Lutherans Meet Head-on

There is a theological fault line that runs through German/ American life, with two massive Teutonic plates scraping by each other, buckling up mountains and barriers, and causing the occasional earthquake that knocks down everything people have built.

The Catholic plate makes up half of all German/Americans. The other half on the other plate are Lutherans. Actually, the Catholics *know* that they should say "Protestant," but they're still blaming Martin Luther for this whole thing.

It stands to reason. Only a *German* could cause this much trouble, while Wycliffe, Knox, Wesley and all the others were just spinning their theological wheels.

There has been a lot of discussion about how disruptive it was for many older Catholics when English replaced Latin in the Mass. But that was nothing compared to the uproar when the priests had to start preaching the homilies in English rather than German.

Nothing upsets a German/American more than something new, particularly something new in church. Some people are still so upset at having to turn around and shake hands with total strangers during the service that they haven't noticed that those liberal ministers have changed the hymnal again.

Other great countries have experimented with religious diversity, notably Ireland, Lebanon and India. But Germany was first, and we called it the Thirty Years' War. Since then we've found that it's more fun arguing with outsiders than with each other, because we know that arguing with another German is like trying to shove the North American continent.

Better Than...
A Pragmatic Theological Comparison

Theologians have debated the fine points of Catholic and Protestant theology for centuries, and frankly, the contest has been pretty much a stand-off.

The point they miss is that few people are swayed by theological arguments, which typically center around words like "hermeneutics," "eschatology" and others that *Reader's Digest* never features in "It Pays to Increase Your Word Power."

Theologians forget that most of us are simply born into, or marry into, a religion. After that, we spend the rest of our lives looking for arguments in our own favor, not comparison-shopping in the Mystical Supermarket.

The hard, unecumenical fact of life is that sharp differences divide German/American Catholics and German/American Lutherans.

There *are* things that Catholics do better than Lutherans, and vice-versa. These are the issues that really *matter* to a churchgoer. Things that can give parishioners a sense of pride seven days a week. Contrast this with unadulterated theology, which makes your stomach hurt when you think about things like what's beyond the outer reaches of the universe.

Here are the differences between German/American Catholics and German/American Lutherans in the *real* world.

Things Catholics Do Better Than Lutherans:

1. **Weddings** — Lutheran weddings are over in 20 minutes. Then the bride and groom shake hands with the guests and everybody leaves. Some good German Catholic wedding dances last nearly as long as some Protestant marriages.

2. **Clothing** — Catholics believe in getting properly dressed up for church. The priest has gorgeous altar vestments with gold brocade, and the altar boys, nuns and the bishop all are dressed to the hilt. To see the Knights of Columbus in full plumage would make you think that the Lord had been a cavalry officer.

3. **Theatrical Churches** — Lutheran churches tend to have the sort of flat, even lighting that one finds in domed stadiums. Catholic churches have dark corners flickering with red votive candles, dramatically lit statues and tiny bells sounding.

4. **Dancing** — If the Lutherans ran Mardi Gras, everybody would wear parkas and go to choir practice instead of parading around half naked, dressed like a Roman Legionette.

5. **Fantasies** — Many a young boy's fantasy life has been given a jump start in parochial school, with all those girls in plaid jumpers and the towering, mysterious, dangerous nuns swooping about. Besides, impure thoughts require less penance than lots of other things.

6. **Spaghetti Suppers** — Protestants may be better at pancake breakfasts, but only Catholics can put on a convincing spaghetti supper. This may be why they call it the *Roman* Catholic church.

7. **Bingo** — Catholics are better at gambling than Lutherans, because Lutherans don't believe there is any such thing as *chance* in either life or religion. While Catholics believe the Lord doesn't frown on gambling as long as it helps the church's work, they *do* believe that the state shouldn't get involved, citing the doctrine of the separation of church and state.

Things Lutherans Do Better Than Catholics:

1. **Singing** — Lutherans sing confidently and lustily because of their centuries of practice and all the great songs they've stolen from the Baptists.

2. **Arguing** — Catholics have only recently realized how invigorating theological infighting can be for a congregation. Lutherans are living proof that synods are the outward and visible sign of an inward and invisible cussedness in congregations.

3. **Youth Groups** — Lutherans confirm their young at the onset of teenage hysteria. This bonding of confirmation with puberty leads naturally to Luther League, the Lutheran expression of the tribal instinct of teenagers. It also makes for an exciting youth group which is only superficially under adult control.

4. **Mission Sundays** — Missionaries were mysterious and entertaining, and could always be counted on to pass around things like dried python skins and poison arrows that no one wanted to touch. The only problem came when they'd try to teach you the Lord's Prayer in Urdu and expect you to remember it an hour later.

5. **Travel** — Religious travel is *serious* business for Catholics. A whole busload of people fingering rosaries on the way to the local shrine where the miracles have not yet been accepted by the hierarchy is bound to be emotionally exhausting.

   Lacking miracles, Lutherans pack up their middle-aged and beyond and ship them off to Germany for a "Cradle of the Reformation Two-Week Tour."

   Two weeks is *way* too long to maintain a white-hot religious fervor. Being Lutheran, these pilgrims never get quite as loose as the pilgrims in *Canterbury Tales*, but the trip does end up feeling like an unchaperoned Luther League convention.

6. **No Confession** — Lutherans don't have confessionals because they never really believe they can be totally

forgiven. They do, however, believe that God occasionally agrees to let some things slide, but that he doesn't like to be reminded of it. This is why Catholics confess things they don't have to confess and Lutherans don't confess things they darn well ought to.

7. **Church League Softball Teams** — While some argue vehemently that Catholics are better athletes because they have natural rhythm, the Lutherans are the ones who win the softball games. This is because Catholics get an earlier start on the respectability of family life and are home caring for kids during their athletic prime, while Lutherans tend to defer fatherhood till their knees give out on the diamond.

A Three-Generation Comparison Between German Catholics and German Lutherans

Religion used to be easy to define. If you lived in Cottonwood, Minnesota, for example, and drove a Ford, you were Catholic. Eddie Kleinhopf was the commander of the Knights of Columbus, and his Ford dealership sold Fords to every good Catholic with a reasonable credit rating in the county.

The Lutherans of Cottonwood, on the other hand, drove Dodges, which they bought from Tom Geisthardt of Bethlehem Lutheran. The Baptists and the poor credit risks bought Chevys from Bill Thompson, a Methodist.

That's all gone now. Today the young people drive Hondas and Toyotas, so you don't even know who you should wave at on the highway.

German/Americans think of religion as eternal and un- changing, so it's not surprising they sometimes miss how the practice of religion changes over the generations. Even when they grumble about Masses in English or Lutheran hymnal revisions, they don't realize there are generation gaps that are as big or bigger than denominational differences.

Here's the sort of thing German/American families have to put up with, whatever their religion.

Attitudes About . . .

	CATHOLIC:	LUTHERAN:
RELIGION IN DAILY LIFE	1. Grandma and Grandpa believed every word the priest said, and heaven help you if you ever got smart-mouthed.	1. Grandma and Grandpa believed that both the Bible and the minister were inerrant. Somehow, grandparents and parents were right up there on the inerrancy scale too.
	2. Mom and Dad don't *necessarily* believe everything the priest says. Particularly some of those young hot-shots just out of the seminary.	2. Mom and Dad still think pretty highly of the minister, but he seems to spend a lot of time talking about congregation finances and divestment in South Africa.
	3. The kids show up at Christmas wearing "I SURVIVED CATHOLIC SCHOOL" t-shirts.	3. The kids do parodies of Jimmy Swaggart at Luther League meetings.
MARRIAGE	1. Grandma and Grandpa told their kids not to come home if they married a Lutheran.	1. Grandma and Grandpa told their kids not even to come home if they married a Catholic.
	2. Mom and Dad don't particularly mind their kids dating Lutherans but would really rather they married a Catholic.	2. Mom and Dad would rather have their kids marry a Catholic than join Hare Krishna.
	3. When the kids talk about mixed marriage, they mean between blacks and whites. If only they wouldn't talk about it in front of Grandma and Grandpa!	3. The kids think a mixed marriage is between a male and a female. They consider it one option.
THE CHURCH	1. Grandpa often said that he wished that he had taken a vocation.	1. Grandpa once thought about devoting his life to the church, but was terrified that he would be assigned to a mission and never see home again.
	2. When she was young, Mom dreamed of being a nun just like Sally Field, but, you know, it didn't work out that way, somehow....	2. Dad thought about going to the seminary, but the draft ended before he graduated.
	3. The daughter is talking about turning Episcopalian so she can be a priest.	3. The kids are majoring in television production, so there's still hope that someone in the family might be a preacher.
HAIR	1. Unless Grandpa kept it short, the foreman would squawk. Grandma kept hers braided.	1. Grandpa kept it short so the flax chaff wouldn't get into it. Grandma kept hers braided.
	2. When Dad noticed how visible his bald spot had become, he practically had a fit and cut it really short. Mom got a pixie cut in college and has stayed with it since then.	2. Both Mom and Dad used to have longer hair, but it kept getting in their eyes during handball.
	3. Their daughter once dyed her hair blue for a party, but washed it all out at a friend's house before going home.	3. Their son once threatened to get a spiked mohawk, but nobody took him seriously.

	CATHOLIC:	LUTHERAN:
PREMARITAL SEX	1. In Grandma's day, nobody much talked about it, but it happened.	1. In Grandma's day, it happened, but nobody *ever* talked about it.
	2. Every Monday morning at school chapel, Sister Sophia used to read the names of parishioners who went to films forbidden by the Legion of Decency.	2. They spent their entire college career wondering: "If this is the sexual revolution, how come I'm spending so many weekends by myself?"
	3. Sister Sophia retired rather than have to teach the AIDS materials at Holy Name High School.	3. It's hard to have a "Birds and Bees" talk with kids who know all the Latin terms, while you know only euphemisms and dirty words.
BABIES	1. The more the better. (What's to stop them, anyway?)	1. The more the better. (Whoever heard of a farm without sons?)
	2. They only wanted a couple, but you wouldn't believe the pressure her mother and her mother-in-law both put on them. She never told either one of them how they managed to stop at three.	2. They planned to have only one child, but everybody told them that only children are always spoiled brats.
	3. One daughter thinks Lamaze is a religion, and you can't shut the other daughter up when she gets on her bandwagon about bringing children into a world with nuclear weapons.	3. Both are so heavily involved with their careers that they have no time to be "into parenting." Despite herself, their mother is about to go buggy, she wants grandchildren so much.
BEER	1. Beer was one of the four basic food groups in Grandma and Grandpa's time. The others were potatoes, bread and meat.	1. Grandpa used to get his bucket of beer after work and bring it home, but Grandma refused to say a word when he did.
	2. Mom and Dad realize that lite beer is better for their waistline, but they just can't get used to the taste.	2. Dad used to have a few when he was in the Air Force, but since he got active in the church again, he only has maybe one at a picnic or something.
	3. The kids went to a kegger in the summer between their eighth and ninth grades and got so sick they swore they'd never touch the stuff again. Pretty much.	3. The kids think beer is for rednecks in pickups with gun racks.
WHO WAS THE FAMILY HERO?	1. Sister Benedicta, Grandma's sister, who had such beautiful penmanship.	1. Grandma's cousin Emil, who had the biggest farm and the tidiest farmyard in three counties.
	2. Uncle Carl, who was the first G.I. across the Rhine.	2. Uncle Otto, who bought the rural telephone company in the '40s, and got so rich you wouldn't believe it, except he never changed. He was an usher at church till the end.
	3. Cousin Tony, whose band is so famous he's played in Holiday Inns all over the country.	3. Uncle Larry, who worked in a mental hospital instead of going to Vietnam.

QUICK! WHICH ONE'S CATHOLIC? WHICH ONE'S LUTHERAN?

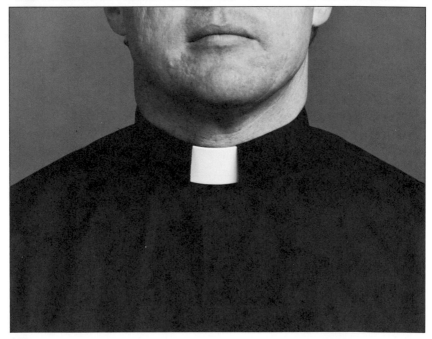

By Their Collars
Shall Ye Know Them:
Identifying the Brave New World of Clerical Diversity

When I was a lad in the old Pre-Vatican Council days, life was simple. My hometown was half Lutheran, half Catholic, with about 19 Episcopalians thrown in for leavening. All we had to do was tell the difference between a Lutheran clerical collar and a Catholic clerical collar.

The frightening thing was, we could do it. We could spot a collar at 50 paces and know unfailingly whether it was attached to a father or a pastor.

Those were the days when there was only one model of everything. One 1956 Chevrolet, one 1956 Ford. One 1956 priest, one 1956 Protestant.

Since then, there has been an explosion of clergy. People now identify themselves as having a clown ministry or a biker ministry, instead of simply crushing your hand and saying, "I'm the new Lutheran youth minister," or "I'm Father Himmelgruber from Our Lady of Immaculate Living Rooms Parish."

Even the most active parishioners can get so caught up in committee work that they fail to notice the changes in their church. I'd like to present a quick guide to the new world of clerical diversity.

From Pope John to Jim and Tammy Faye

Pastor Reinking has begun to think it would be easier to bridge the gap between low church and high church if it weren't for the tigers on both ends of the bridge.

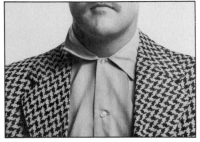

Pastor Dauer was convinced that the snooty clergy in the downtown churches just hated him because he wore a $20 shirt, a $7 tie and $500 alligator shoes, and told the *truth* about the gospel.

After years on the revival circuit warning of the wrath of God, Earl Pelzl found he rather *preferred* wrath to grace as a sermon topic.

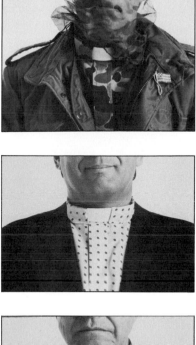

Already famous for his sermon "Nobody Would Have Crucified Jesus if He'd Been Properly Armed," Rev. Zwangl personally led his flock in stockpiling six months' dried food and first-aid supplies in their reinforced church basement.

Although he was an expert administrator, many felt that Pastor Schmitz's habit of wearing a "power collar" after he received his M.B.A. was a little too yuppified.

Many in the congregation felt that Reverend Steiner's attitudes were more Calvinist than Lutheran, and the rumor grew that he had actually been born in Glasgow.

Reverend Windschitl's habit of saying "On the other hand…" won him the unofficial title of the Non-denominational, Fully Ecumenical, Generical Clerical.

Pastor Holzberger had been sent to convert the Episcopalians of Kennebunkport to Lutheranism, but was recalled when the bishop feared that he had 'gone native.'

Hans Pfandlsteiner had always wanted to be a missionary, but he never could stand the prickly heat.

Peter and Paul Herrendoerfer, the twin brothers who became Fathers, started a ministry to twins and received some notoriety when they referred to the Trinity as "the Holy Triplets."

Charles Grunst had expected to be able to take the hell out of the Hell's Angels with his biker ministry, but was shocked to find little acceptance among the outlaw set.

Father Zangel works behind the scenes of Las Vegas shows, hearing confessions from showgirls who *definitely* are not wearing something to cover their heads.

Those Lutherans who expect their pastors to be grey-haired old men named Fortwengler are going to need some midcourse corrections.

Father Schapekahm has ministered to souls in America's trailer parks so long that he no longer feels comfortable in any kitchen that doesn't rock.

Reverend Niehoff obviously does not believe that clown ministries are the male equivalent of theological interpretive dance and every bit as annoying.

Working with the beach people of Southern California, Reverend Kupferschmidt in time became known as the Chippendale Chaplain.

Few people realize the tremendous pressure the Super Bowl Chaplain is under, counseling half-time singers and dancers overcome by stage fright.

Nothing in his career had prepared Father Zumhofe for the sort of control the hostile new parish board expected to have on his ministry.

Father Prahl found the transition to the Episcopalian clergy smoother than expected, despite certain distractions.

After years of seeing most of his congregation only at Christmas and Easter, Reverend Gerhard Hinnenthal finally became re-signed to the situation.

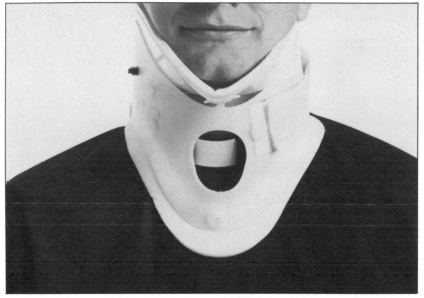

Father Lietzau has had some time to regret his decision to cancel the weekly bingo games in his parish.

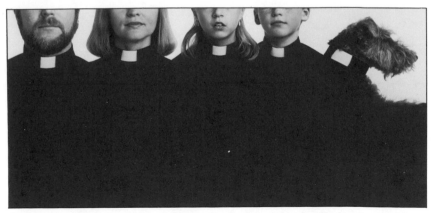

Although only the pastor gets a paycheck, the entire family is expected to work for free and engage only in above-average conduct.

It's safe to assume that if he starts devotions with "Awright, lissen up," he's the youth pastor.

It was widely assumed that Reverend Weicherding chose a trip to the seminary instead of a trip to Vietnam.

Pastor Schleggelmilch had always been content as the music minister at Living Word Lutheran until the Nashville Gospel Evangelists came through town.

Uncertain of whether he would catch flak from the right wing or the left wing of his congregation for any given deed, Father Muhlbauer began to develop a serious tic.

Instead of five strong men each contributing a unique viewpoint, the pastoral committee quickly degenerated into a pack with an Alpha male and a four-man Amen Corner.

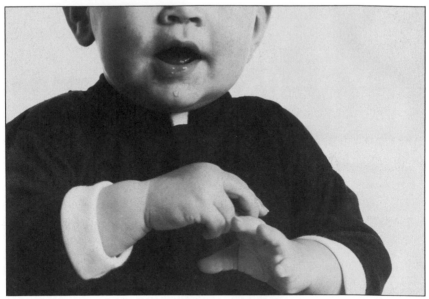

Everybody agreed that the man was a born preacher.

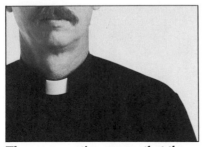

The congregation agrees that the pastor is *way* too far to the left.

Some special-interest types in the congregation think the pastor might be a little too far to the right.

Not everyone in the congregation appreciated the close watch Father Zusamenschneider kept on his flock.

Some suggested that Pastor Kirschbaum's fiery sermons and vivid imagery may have had something to do with his fondness for the occasional glass.

The search committee today reported that none of the new candidates measured up to their high standards any more than the minister they just fired.

The Annual Blessing of the Snowmobiles wasn't something Father Schlosser had looked forward to when he was transferred to Minnesota from Louisiana.

The entire congregation devoutly hopes that the new minister will grow into the job.

Reverend Rengstorf's midlife crisis started when he realized that he was a counter-culture clerical caught in the conservative counter-revolution.

Pastor Plumhoff, the Potluck Padre, a priest who's prayed at one too many picnics.

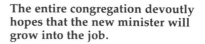

After six months of hosting "Footprints in the Sands of Time" for public-access cable TV, Pastor Pahmeier had to admit that he felt a little bit like a celebrity.

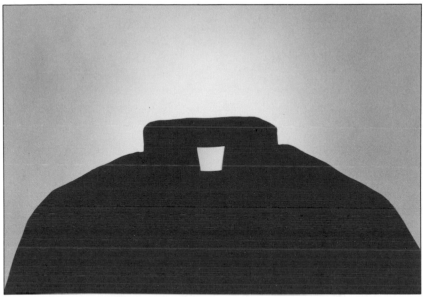

Every new pastor at Divine Grace Lutheran Church soon discovers that the congregation places more faith in the office itself than in the office-holder.

The old prison chaplain may now be the chaplain prisoner: proof that both the times and legal accounting standards change.

NINJA WORRIER TOURNAMENT TO BE OPEN TO PUBLIC

Shaun Schoenbechler has become Wisconsin's first German/American Ninja Worrier, having achieved the highest level of anxiety in the Way of the Worrier, an ancient Eastern religion that stresses the moral value of staying awake nights, developing bleeding ulcers and reading too much news.

The five levels of anxiety consciousness in the Way of the Worrier are: 1. Nervous, 2. Knotted, 3. Hysterical, 4. Suicidal, and for those who progress beyond, 5. the Ultimate, the All-Seeing Phobic-Master.

Although he's terrified that he could lose his whole life savings in this deal, Shaun plans to open a series of tacky storefront Ninja Worrier schools where he will teach the Way of the Worrier to marginally paranoid suburban housewives and be treated like a big shot by confused adolescents.

100 Years of Rectitude:
Propriety as Chief Virtue

Everybody grows up with parents who worry about what the neighbors will think about what they've done. German/Americans have parents who worry about what the neighbors will think about what they *haven't* done.

It's not enough to get through high school without getting arrested. That would be too easily verifiable a standard to live up to. We wouldn't want our kids getting lazy and smug just because they're not axe murderers.

So we worry about things that don't happen: "What will the neighbors think if you *don't* get the scholarship?" In reality, all the neighbors are thinking about is what *you're* thinking about their children.

What nobody tells you is that in 20 years, your whole childhood — good, bad or indifferent — will be balanced on a fulcrum of "and/but."

If you were famous around the block for acting out, acting up and throwing down the gauntlet, in 20 years all they'll say is, "Well, he was pretty wild when he was in school, *BUT* he's calmed down and doing pretty good now." Or they'll say, "He was a wild kid, *AND* he's still a pain in the neck." Everything's connected. You can't escape.

What this leads to is the idea that we are always a disappointment to everyone and that embarrassment is synonymous with reality. When we finally do something good, we're among the first to point it out, because that sort of thing can get lost.

Embarrassment as a Team Sport

German/Americans see reflections everywhere. You are a reflection on everybody to whom you are related, know or live near, and they, in turn, are all reflections on you.

What's amazing is how much embarrassment and how little glory is reflected. German/Americans believe that "basking in reflected glory" is just a nice way of saying that you are an idle hanger-on.

Being embarrassed is a concrete and tangible experience we all have known. German/Americans know that life is hard. If your life isn't, go back and check your data: You've probably overlooked something.

We help our friends by reminding them of things they should be embarrassed about. German/Americans prefer embarrassment to guilt because guilt is a private game that can be played by only one or two at a time. Embarrassment, on the other hand, requires whole teams. It's practically a tournament sport for us. Embarrassment is collective. Everybody can play, and everybody usually does.

Every good game needs a scorecard. How embarrassed can you *really* feel until you've had your little problem quantified, graphed and publicly analyzed? How can you take pride in your shame without knowing how you scored, vis-a-vis your friends?

By charting your embarrassment, you remove the sting and make even the worst situation seem logical, rational and linear. By assigning numbers, you make it a competitive event.

Here are a few of the major embarrassment charts for our lives, taking you from your first all the way through to your second childhood. Get a sharp #2 pencil and fill out these charts for yourself. Or use an ink pen so you can't erase and make it easy on yourself.

Enjoy! And watch yourself!

Elementary School Embarrassment

Elementary school is a particularly fertile time for embarrassment. You don't know the rules yet, and nobody will tell you. (Note to teachers and parents: "DON'T!" is not a *rule*. It is a *challenge*.)

Here are some things you can do that will reflect shame on your family and friends while you are still in grade school.

1. Having milk shoot out your nose when you laugh at dinner
2. Eating cookie dough
3. Chewing your fingernails and swallowing them
4. Biting a blister to see what it tastes like
5. Swallowing gum
6. Swallowing toothpaste
7. Climbing trees
8. Climbing cliffs
9. Riding a bike with no hands
10. Smoking cigarettes

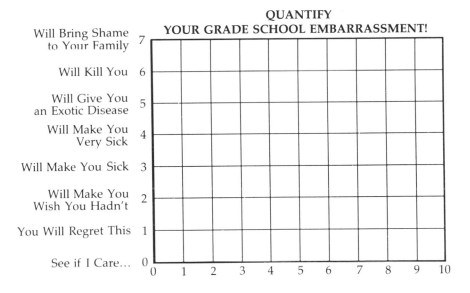

QUANTIFY YOUR GRADE SCHOOL EMBARRASSMENT!

Will Bring Shame to Your Family	7
Will Kill You	6
Will Give You an Exotic Disease	5
Will Make You Very Sick	4
Will Make You Sick	3
Will Make You Wish You Hadn't	2
You Will Regret This	1
See if I Care...	0

High School Embarrassment

This is the big leagues of embarrassment. Being seen with your parents can cause clinical depression in one out of four junior high students. Everything's embarrassing, because they still won't tell you what the rules are, and they've stopped yelling "DON'T!" and are now yelling "STOP IT!!"

1. Not making the team
2. Letting things "get out of hand" when you're parking
3. Getting pregnant
4. Getting someone else pregnant
5. Drinking in high school
6. Drinking more than your parents do
7. Getting kicked off the team for drinking
8. Failing a class
9. Being snubbed by someone of the opposite sex
10. Having your parents called to the principal's office

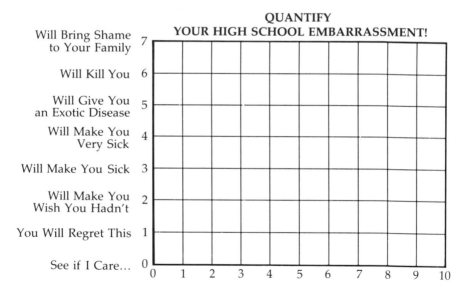

Life-Long Embarrassment

You'd think that when you graduated and became financially independent, you'd finally be a good reflection on everybody. You're working, or married, or both, so at least your mother can stop worrying.

But now you've got a boss and a spouse to reflect your embarrassment, and you really *are* old enough to know better.

1. Having an unmowed lawn
2. Keeping junk in the yard
3. Giving a guest a plate with a goober the dishwasher missed
4. Not shaving and wearing dirty clothes on vacation
5. Leaving papers and underwear all over the house
6. Missing an appointment with a client
7. Getting fired
8. Living together
9. Having an affair
10. Getting divorced

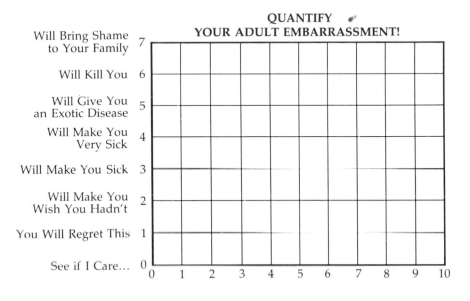

QUANTIFY YOUR ADULT EMBARRASSMENT!

Will Bring Shame to Your Family — 7
Will Kill You — 6
Will Give You an Exotic Disease — 5
Will Make You Very Sick — 4
Will Make You Sick — 3
Will Make You Wish You Hadn't — 2
You Will Regret This — 1
See if I Care... — 0

0 1 2 3 4 5 6 7 8 9 10

Being Graded by Your Children

You can't outlive your critics. When your parents start spending most of their day looking for their false teeth and claiming that they've been stolen by communists, your own kids start keeping tabs on you.

Just to keep you on your toes, here's how you can reflect embarrassment on the younger generation.

1. Lip-syncing "Like a Virgin" in front of their friends
2. Showing their teenage friends your kids' baby pictures
3. Commenting publicly on rock 'n' roll
4. Trying to make a joke when you meet their teacher
5. Commenting on their weight gain
6. Talking loudly about other people in public
7. Taking in six cats when your spouse dies
8. Remarrying at age 70
9. Refusing to go to a nursing home when it's clear to your kids that you need to
10. Signing over your will to a TV evangelist

From Science Fair to Ego Fair

All high school reunions resemble each other because they're all run by former cheerleaders and student-government types. Those folks run the reunions like they ran high school — in their own image.

However, when the 20th reunion of the Sherman Adams High School, Class of 1964, rolled around, the senior-class president was under indictment for insider trading in pork-bellies futures and the entire cheerleading squad had joined a lesbian mime collective. They responded to the invitation by sending a communiqué denouncing the bourgeois sensibilities of their classmates and the repressive educational system that produced them, but offering to perform one of their shows.

Under these trying circumstances, the job of organizing the reunion was left to Bill Schretzenmayer, who was still famous among his classmates for winning the science fair four years in a row. In fact, winning the science fair was the *only* thing most of his classmates could remember about Bill.

It shouldn't have come as a surprise to anyone that the reunion Bill organized re-created his own high school triumphs. He approached the problem like a science fair project, surveying the relevant data in various journals and concluding that there were three primary reasons for attending a high school reunion. In order of importance, they were:

1. Bragging;
2. Getting drunk;
3. Attempting to consummate an unconsummated teenage romance.

Since Bill couldn't believe that point three applied to *his* high school classmates, and since he knew all too well that they would take care of point two by themselves, he decided to concentrate on the first point.

Bill quickly realized that a major bottleneck in reunions was the lack of an efficient Affirmative Information Dispersal Module. In the traditional reunion module, people have to wait for someone to ask whether they have gotten rich or raised

Mrs. Brenda Uttenreuther (nee Geilersdorfer) joins Eldon Lyle Pfletschinger at the Sherman Adams High School 20th Reunion Ego Fair.

Eldon won first place for his Bragging Booth presentation titled "My Way," which documented his rise in the business world and achievements in many other areas of life. Eldon's classmates should know that he now prefers to be addressed only as "E.L." or "Fletch."

Brenda has been active in the art world since she was president of Future Hobbyists of America at SAHS. She has won many awards at county and state fairs in the fields of decoupage, rug hooking, string art and greenware. Currently she is employed designing paint-by-number kits for velvet paintings.

overachieving children. But in reality, the three most commonly asked questions at reunions are:

1. "Bar still open?"
2. "You still married to, you know...?"
3. "Where's the little girl's room?"

Another critical issue was misinterpretation of data. What

incentive would a woman have to wear a Christian Lacroix dress if only half the women and none of the men knew the difference between raw silk and rayon?

Finally, there was the issue of ambiguity. If your classmates think that the fast track is a county road the sheriff never patrols, you can't expect them to grasp the full impact of your rise from CFO to CEO.

What was required to address these problems was a system whereby a person's achievements could be arranged in a logical sequence, displayed graphically for all to see, and presented in a pleasing manner.

In short, Bill created the concept of an Ego Fair, complete with Bragging Booths.

The idea was a smashing success. Attendance rose 23.7 percent over the previous reunion record, and the local cable TV station covered the fair, featuring it on the "Purina Neighbor of the Week" show.

Disappointing Your Parents

Sooner or later, we all disappoint our parents. They disappoint us too, but since they will always be older than we are, it doesn't count.

Disappointing your parents is a uniquely human activity. Salmon are pretty good parents, I suppose, but they don't even expect all 10,000 eggs to hatch, let alone expect them all to become internists with a good practice.

German/Americans have raised disappointing your parents to the level of a performance art. As children, we instinctively know that there are *standards*; that there are *expectations*. Our parents expect us to live up to standards. *Their* standards, generally speaking.

Sometimes, we get this crazy notion that we can actually please our parents. But parents have a way of moving the target. For example: Imagine the frustration of spending your life pleasing your mother by getting a Ph.D. and achieving tenure in a major research university, only to find that your mother has changed her mind, and now wishes you had become a hell-fire preacher in a storefront church instead.

Expectations, like prayers, have the unfortunate habit of coming true, usually in a clumsy sort of way that spotlights what we were *really* asking for.

Here is some of the trauma created by living out someone else's *traum* (dream).

1. *TRAUM*:
   My daughter is the most popular girl in her class.
   TRAUMA:
   Hyper-popular, socially precocious young women — even today — have the unnerving habit of becoming pregnant by the *strangest* partners.

2. *TRAUM*:
   My son is an All-Conference jock.
   TRAUMA:
   Astonishingly, there still are parents who push their sons into a sports career so the kids won't get involved with drugs.

3. *TRAUM*:
   My very feminine daughter wins her first beauty-queen title at age 4.
   TRAUMA:
   The pages of *Penthouse* and *Playboy* are filled monthly with young women who have grown quite adept at trading on their beauty and femininity.

4. *TRAUM*:
   My son makes us all proud by becoming a doctor.
   TRAUMA:
   If you base the family status on Junior's M.D., what happens if he gets convicted of bilking Medicaid patients?

5. *TRAUM*:
   My child grows up to become a teacher.

TRAUMA:
Even a Teacher of the Year can get fired during budget cuts if he or she has less seniority than some fossil.

6. *TRAUM:*
All my children get married.
TRAUMA:
Married is good, but not if it's too soon, or to the wrong spouse, or into the wrong religion, and *certainly* not if it leads to divorce. Better endure the shame of having them live together.

7. *TRAUM:*
All my children are very devout.
TRAUMA:
The emphatically religious often find their way to storefront churches or even to out-and-out cults. Even if they stay good Catholic (or Lutheran) kids, they could become so holy that they start commenting unfavorably on *your* behavior.

8. *TRAUM:*
My children all work hard and get high-powered jobs.
TRAUMA:
Someone with a fast-track job will spend most of his/her life at the office, with little time left for visits to the old folks at home.

9. *TRAUM:*
Be happy.
(As in "All I want for you is ...")
TRAUMA:
What good is it having kids who are so pleased with themselves that they lacked the fire in the gut to make something big of themselves?

10. *TRAUM:*
Give me some grandchildren!
TRAUMA.
But not if they're loud, or break things, or dress in ways I dislike.

ATHLETIC OVERACHIEVERS OVER-RECOGNIZED

Germans pump up their egos by awarding themselves titles. One is known as Frau Professor Gstattenbauer or Herr Intendant Schneidkraut. Titles are seldom used in the United States, so we German/Americans pump up our egos by awarding trophies that are totally inappropriate to the level of achievement.

At the left is Hilarian "Bud" Zipfl, the 1989 Northwestern Stearns County Bowler of the Year.

At the right is Chuck Zitzelsberger, winner of the 1989 Burr Oaks Sports & Yacht Club Spring Racquetball Tournament, 25-35 year age bracket, men's division.

Bud's five-foot trophy now has a place of honor in the entryway to his mobile home. Chuck and his wife, Cindy, are saving the bottle of port he won as an element of their investment-grade-beverage portfolio.

A Progress Report on Utopia

During the last century, many Germans moved to America because their neighbors had just about had it with them. German immigrants often were utopians, which means they took everything seriously and argued with anyone who didn't take things seriously.

What utopians call "seizing the moral high ground" others call "being a troublemaker." Our ancestors were continually seizing the moral high ground by arguing with the parish priest, the army recruiting officer and various civil authorities.

Realizing that they had pushed their luck about as far as it would go, our ancestors decided to move to America because "Emigrant" sounded like a much better job classification than "Prisoner."

Because they were Germans first and utopians second, the first thing our ancestors did when they hit the frontier was to establish a brewery. Occasionally provisions were made for storing grain and laying out streets, but one gets the impression that it was only because they realized they couldn't deliver the beer if there weren't enough streets.

Once the first crop of hops fermented adequately and everybody had a taste, they sat down in their new streets and had themselves a good boo-hoo about the old country. There is nothing more sentimental than an immigrant who was forced to leave his or her country.

We have discarded the utopian ideals of our ancestors because we have found that utopias don't work unless they're inhabited by saints, and saints don't get to drink beer. We have, however, maintained our German heritage in some unique ways. This chapter is a quick look at some of those ways.

· Deutschneyland:
A Theme Park for Grim Youngsters

A theme is what passes for thought among people with very short attention spans. This explains theme restaurants, which don't want you spending much time thinking about the quality of their food.

While this trend originally was isolated among desperate restaurateurs, the contagion has been spreading. Whole geographic areas are now at theme-risk.

There are World War theme parks for the passive-aggressive to stroll, while hostile-aggressives can run around special wooded areas "killing" each other with paint pellets. If this is still too tame, you can go to a Survivalist theme camp and learn to kill your fellow men without the quotation marks.

If this trend continues, we soon shall have theme countries. "Six Theologies over Ruritania" would be a lively place, particularly if they armed the truth-seekers and let them have at it in public. Iran, Lebanon and Ireland are already part of this franchise.

Donald Trump, Leona Helmsley and Oliver North could establish "Gimme-Land" on an unnamed Caribbean island. The kiddies could ride the dizzying International Currency Fluctuator, and then clean up in the Money Laundry, where the faucets are on the ceiling because everybody knows the Trickle-down Theory is the only free-market answer. Anybody who asked where the planeloads of money came from would automatically be sent to Disappeared-Land.

The most recent entry into the theme-park competition was unveiled this week by Inter/Multi, a large (and somewhat shadowy) holding company based in Minneapolis but incorporated under the more lenient tax laws of Switzerland. Inter/Multi is making a truly international effort to provide American families the newest, brightest entertainment opportunities.

To this international end, Inter/Multi has brought in financing from a consortium of Japanese, Hong Kong and Singapore banks, hired a famous Italian design firm and retained a multi-national public relations firm headquartered in London.

Flanked by a bipartisan delegation of local and state officials at the initial press conference, the CEO of Inter/Multi promised the park would provide several hundred jobs for American construction workers and "just a whole lot" of continuing jobs within the park itself. Many of these jobs are certain to be above minimum wage.

The officials expressed confidence that there would be no problem getting the special tax-increment financing demanded by Inter/Multi through the state legislature to make this exciting new family project possible. "When we said the word 'family,' every politician in the room went down on one knee and bowed their heads," Inter/Multi's chief political strategist explained. "We've got these suckers locked up."

OVERLEAF: Ground was broken today for *DEUTSCHNEYLAND,* America's only family amusement park based on polka and beer. *DEUTSCHNEYLAND* will employ 500 people at some time in the future and provide family entertainment for the whole family.

Present at the ground-breaking were, from left to right, Frank Loeffelmacher, concrete and steel supervisor, Himmelhuber Brothers Construction; George Himmelhuber, president, Himmelhuber Brothers Construction; Toshihiko Nishiguchi, Osaka Bank and Trust; Chen Yingqiang, Hong Kong Investment, Ltd.; Jiang Shoubin, Merchants Marine Trust, Singapore; Bill Thompson, CEO, Inter/Multi, Inc.; Tom Hennings, CFO, Inter/Multi, Inc.; Cari Carr, Vice President, community relations, Inter/Multi, Inc. ▶

DEUTSCHNEYLAND™

DEUTSCHNEYLAND™ is Family Entertainment for the Whole Family! Located in the rolling hills and valleys of central Minnesota. **DEUTSCHNEYLAND™** is the place you want to bring your Family for a full day of Family Fun with a Teutonic flair! Bring your wallet and celebrate your heritage till you're oom-pahed out!

BIERGARTEN LAND—Right in the midst of America's "Shining Waves of Hops," our Biergarten will make you think you're back in Munich, whether or not you've ever been to Germany. Stay a little longer and you won't know *where* you are, but you'll have done your part in upholding your German/American traditions!

POLKA LAND—Polka till you plop! The best polka party in the U.S.A.! Run by the man responsible for the famous three-day Daglish-Gatzlaff wedding party at St. Mary's Parish in Cincinnati back in 1962! Adjacent chiropractor's office for those who can't keep up.

OVERACHIEVER LAND—A favorite for kids of all ages! See how *you* measure up, and decide what you are going to do about it.

WIRTSCHAFTSWUNDER LAND—What's the economic incentive to beat your swords into plowshares when the Middle East isn't desperate for farming equipment?

Learn about balance of payments, economic miracles, and trading something more interesting than baseball cards. No need to stand in line—we'll handle you quickly and discreetly.

HISTORY LAND—Also known as NOSTALGIA LAND: where farming can make you rich, or even solvent!

Watch the Grand Parade of Progress where small towns follow the farmers follow the cowboys into oblivion!

SPACE LAND—From V-2 to Star Wars, America's SPACE LAND is, has been and always will be brought to you by German/American scientists who have *conquered their accents!*
PRETEND LAND—TWO parks in one! Mom and Dad get to climb into the back seat of a two-toned pastel '58 Buick and have the tackiest of tanta-sies about being back in high school.

Meanwhile, Junior and Sis trot off to the Juggernaut, where state-of-the-art computer graphics provide all the sensations of watching their parents being eaten alive by bloodthirsty dinosaurs, or fill their fantasies of demolishing schools with large, deadly space-alien military vehicles.

EATING YOUR WAY AROUND
DEUTSCHNEYLAND™

What fun is a large concrete amusement park without lots of opportunities to eat food that's bad for you? **DEUTSCHNEYLAND**™ has *lots and lots* of fun food booths! You'll never be far from one of these great taste treats: **KARAMEL KRAUT**—A unique, German/American Sweet 'n' Sour treat. You'll *never* forget it! **BITTY BRATS**—Little, tiny wieners so you have to buy lots of them even for the littlest appetite! **DEEP-FRIED SPAETZLE**—Teenagers will love it! High in carbohydrates, salt and, best of all, *you can eat it with your fingers!*

THE HASENPFEFFER HUT—Give the kids $50 and go have a nice meal with the wife. The menu is entirely in German, so the squeamish won't get upset about what they're eating. **SCHNITZEL ON A STICK**—If you're a "gotta go! gotta go!" type person, you can get a good meal and still keep up with the kids! **THE TORTE TENT**—Take a load off your feet and put it on your thighs. Forever. Nothing in the world compares to Black Forest torte, at least nothing that's legal! *Alles schmeckt gut!*

------------------------------✂------------

Stop Feeling So Good About Yourself!

German/Americans are deeply suspicious of people who spend a lot of time feeling good about themselves. We hold to the notion that there is a finite supply of goodness in the world, and that those who have it don't squander it by talking about it.

Like patriotism, feeling good about yourself has become a scoundrel's refuge. We are expected to applaud the insight of some S.O.B. who asks forgiveness (without offering a refund) after cheating us on a business deal because he "is still working through a lot of personal issues." This is like asking us to applaud Charles Manson for feeling good about himself because recently he's been sticking to a regular program of dental hygiene.

We believe that darn few people really deserve to feel good about themselves. Meanwhile, the ones who shouldn't feel good about themselves, but do, are causing problems like this.

What Has Feeling Good About Ourselves Brought Us?

1. Middle-aged men in bikini underwear.
2. Women who wear full eye make-up to aerobics classes hoping to meet available men.
3. Guests on TV talk shows who air their sexual dysfunctions as though they were admirable achievements.
4. Couples who dress alike in public.
5. People who go around saying "I'm O.K., you're O.K." when *we* know very well that they're not!
6. Women who wear a mink coat over a sweat suit to go to the grocery store.
7. People who are *proud* that they are politically correct.
8. Teenage boys in pickups with jacked-up suspensions and oversized tires.
9. Models, mimes and "performance" artists.

10. People who wear all their jewelry to the pool instead of putting it in the hotel safe.
11. Former administration officials caught with their fingers in the cookie jar who have "found the Lord." Was he hiding from everybody, or just them?
12. Ministers who aren't embarrassed when their doomsday prophecies keep needing to be rescheduled.

State Fairs:
Body Contact for the Claustrophobic

Every healthy person establishes psychological boundaries to protect himself. German/Americans are the only people who maintain customs and passport control booths at these boundaries.

Those who study proxemics tell us that Northern Europeans, particularly Germans, require far larger zones of personal space than do people from other cultures. People from various Latin cultures, for instance, are comfortable standing much closer to each other than Germans are. Perhaps this is because *all* the Latinos ate garlic at lunch, so no one feels conspicuous.

German/Americans have inherited this need for personal space. If you don't believe me, walk into the Farmers' Grain Elevator in Wilton Junction, Iowa, and keep walking till you're toe to toe with some old farmer you've never met before. It will be a real laugh riot, I promise you. If those old farmers *wanted* you to get that close, they wouldn't have grown their bumper bellies to keep you at your distance.

Just don't walk up to some young guy like that. He'll probably think you're the new loan officer at the Tipton Bank come for his farm loan. You'll soon find out that the danger in invading someone's personal space is that it's hard to retreat quickly.

But even German/Americans get lonely, secure as we are in our impregnable personal-space fortresses. We tire of farm towns with streets wider than the Champs Elysees and emptier than a Beirut tourist hotel. We get restless with the prairie,

On the rare occasions when Germans and Austrians let down their guard and implode their personal-space requirements, the result is dramatic. Here the entire population of Vienna's Old Town has decided to stand in the same tiny *Platz* so they can drink *Gluhwein* and absorb a year's worth of body contact in one winter afternoon.

where even the landscape doesn't crowd you. We want human contact. We want to feel a little, well, pregnable.

But we want *controlled* contact. Safe contact. Anonymous contact. A place where we can make contact without having to, you know, *connect*. It's no fluke that German/Americans prefer dating in automobiles. Sitting in the front seat of a car, you can't be *expected* to maintain eye contact with the other person. Eye contact between German/Americans tends to degenerate into a game of "who blinked first" and may be too intense for first dates anyway.

So how do we German/Americans fill our need for human contact? We get our contact fairly. We go to fairs.

We love fairs because we can pack away our claustrophobia and rub shoulders (and elbows, and thighs, and bellies) with thousands of other people wearing double-knit bermuda shorts. The problem with surrendering your identity and joining a crowd is that you do things your ethics and aesthetics normally would forbid.

In other words, we *use* fairs for our own wicked ends. Fairs provide excuses to indulge in behaviors that our friends frown on. We go to fairs so we can't help ourselves.

For example: Bob Schwinkerdorf, who works at the New Horizon Health Foods Co-op, eats so healthfully that you'd think he planned to outlive the Trinity. But once a year, Bob schlumps off to the Minnesota State Fair and eats miniature doughnuts, large buckets of french fries where the grease congeals before you finish, deep-fried cheese-on-a-stick, and chocolate-covered bananas. *Bob can't help himself!*

Mary Pfarrdrescher is an interior designer who specializes in postmodern loft spaces. Every third year, she weakens and goes to the Renaissance Fair, where she becomes at one with the ambience and the crowd. Inevitably, Mary buys a large, dark-leather and wood plant-hanger/mirror which the artist has christened "The Lord of the Rings Biospace." *Mary can't help herself!*

All this human contact makes us a little giddy and lowers our resistance to ideas we have spent years outgrowing. Bob grew up in the Twinkie Generation, but he has reformed. Mary grew up dangerously close to a trailer court that housed southern Minnesota's largest collection of Sad Clown paintings.

But it's a small price to pay for a little annual human contact. It's warm and comforting to be in a crowd so thick that you could lift your feet and not fall down. It's hard not to feel *connected* when only sex offers greater physical contact.

And it's genuinely innocent. It's not like those midwestern hot-tub parties where they invite only married couples and everybody makes a big deal of announcing beforehand that *they'll* be wearing swimsuits. That's just impure thinking masquerading as progressive behavior.

The German language, once mastered, can
prove a powerful tool for the communication of abstract
philosophical concepts, the discussion of state-of-the-art technological
issues, and the analysis and judgment of other people's behavior.

Sprechen Sie?
American Damage to the Mother Tongue

A mericans don't learn foreign languages because it's too far. We live too far away from people who speak other languages to keep from getting rusty. It's not like Europe where you don't know what language to apologize in if you bump into someone.

If each of our 50 states spoke a separate language, this argument goes, Americans would be linguists. If Iowa spoke a different language, for instance, Minnesotans would probably learn it, if only as a party joke. But if South Dakota were a foreign country, it would likely be in the Third World, so Minnesotans *still* wouldn't learn their language.

German/Americans don't think of German as a foreign language. They think of it as a guilt trip. Either we should have paid better attention to Grandma, or we should have paid attention in school, because if we had, we'd know it now.

But language classes in schools are about as useful as prisons that teach convicts how to make automobile license plates. Granted, it's a skill, but it's nothing you'd use to spark up your résumé.

You must also remember that the German language is a dangerous language. *Du* and *Sie* both mean "you," but you can get in deep doo-doo with *Du*. Don't ask why. It's just the way they are over there.

I've tried to address all these issues and more in this chapter. Tape cassettes of these language lessons soon will be available. In the meantime, just point and grin.

The Case Against International Understanding

International understanding is a wonderful thing. Who can forget Ronald Reagan's joy when he discovered on his first South American trip as President of the United States that "they're all separate countries down there!" That's the sort of little epiphany for which every traveler prays.

But international understanding is a rare commodity and ought to be reserved for national policy-makers and ruthless business types. People with lots of international understanding know exactly how much bauxite Quasistan produces. They even know what bauxite is good for.

Frighteningly, they also know that Quasistan has dangerous enemies — evil people who would restrict the flow of bauxite to the free world unless the U.S. military intervenes *this very afternoon*!

That's the sort of nonsense that international understanding has brought us. There are those who would argue that every citizen should be encyclopedically informed so we can counter self-serving arguments like this. But Americans can't even decide whether lite beer tastes great or is less filling. You can't expect people like that to make it through a bauxite production schedule.

The second good bit of news for travelers is that the Ugly American cliché is dead. Ever since the dollar became as valuable as a warehouse full of Mondale for President bumper stickers, the Ugly American tourist has been replaced by Ugly Japanese tourists, Ugly German tourists, Really Ugly British sports fan tourists, and so on.

There is a shop in Heidelberg selling Hummel figurines, Steuben glass and nutcrackers, where all the signs are in Japanese. The Oslo airport gift shop has Arabic signs for the more upscale items. Mexican hotel workers take evening lessons in the German language, if not German punctuality.

The geographical isolation of the United States works

against international understanding. Therefore, I'm unilaterally declaring an end to international understanding. It never really worked, and Lord knows, Americans never took much of an interest in it.

Perhaps the best part is that if we don't need international understanding, we certainly don't need to learn any foreign languages, and the United States already leads the world in not learning foreign languages. It's nice to know that our country is #1 in something again!

Don't Learn the Language

We force our youth into language classes by saying another language will be useful to them in later life. If that were true, we'd teach our kids Japanese so they could read the owner's manuals for their cars, TV's, stereos and VCR's.

Then we tell our young scholars another joke. We tell them that when they actually need to speak the language, "it" will all come back to them. The amazing thing is that young people never see through this joke. It should be apparent to them that if "it" doesn't come back to them in a test they've crammed for up to 20 minutes ago, "it" isn't likely to come back to them 20 years later either.

I speak from the most horrific personal experience. After four years of German, the only "it" that ever came back to me was panic. Panic was my constant emotional state in German class. When I got off the plane in Frankfurt and walked up to the car rental, "it" came back. Immediately. Perfectly. I was absolutely fluent in panic. I remembered *everything* about my German classes. Who sat next to me. Whom I dated, and whom I wished I could have dated. How long and cold the silences were when I was called on for an answer. Only pronunciation, syntax, vocabulary and verb declensions were missing from my memory.

The panic attack passed. I started to breathe in shallow, careful gasps, as if I were about to give birth right there in the Frankfurt airport next to Dr. Mueller's World of Sexy shop.

For the rest of our trip, I would, with fear and trembling, go up to clerks and ask, "Sprechen Sie Englisch...?" They nearly always did, of course, and I was grateful for their weary looks of contempt, because if they didn't, I would be forced to continue in my dime-store Deutsch.

My wife, on the other hand, has never had a German class in her life, so she knows no fear. She would swoop up to a clerk and announce in her most commanding, let's-clear-this-up-right-now tones, "You *do* speak English, don't you?"

On the rare occasion when nobody did speak English, she just handed the ball off to me. I'd listen to five minutes of German gibberish, stare at the price tag, and make a decision entirely on the basis of cost. If it was cheaper to my ego than my pocketbook to escape, I'd buy it and run.

Don't Brush Up Your German

When German/Americans start to plan a trip to Germany, they immediately think of brushing up on their German so they can talk to their relatives. This is as dangerous as being operated on by someone who has only recently "brushed up" on his/her neurosurgical skills. It takes as long to learn German as it does to learn to be a brain surgeon, and requires about the same level of skill.

Why You Shouldn't Bother to Learn German Before Traveling to Germany

- Bargaining is a nonverbal skill, not that any German shopkeepers ever bargain. If you want to bargain with shopkeepers in Germany, study Turkish and shop where the guest workers live.
- Speaking German only encourages people to answer you in German, and you have no idea how fast those people talk!
- What makes you think you'll *want* to talk to your German relatives? These are people who share the same genetic traits that make going to family reunions in America so painful. Let them feed you, then smile at them, nod a lot, and let everything they say flash through your head

without touching a single brain cell. Treat them just like your family at home!

- Consider this: As horrible as visiting the relatives may be, they're bound to be more polite than total strangers. If you become fluent in German, you will be able to understand everything the locals are saying about you as you walk down the street. People treat Americans like they're invisible and say the damnedest things within earshot because they know that virtually no American will understand what they're saying.
- We are told to learn German before we go to Germany so we can be a good guest in their country. Haven't they ever heard about the responsibilities of being a good host and making *us* feel comfortable?
- Germany ranks somewhere in the middle of the gratitude scale. Some countries, like China, are flattered that dunderhead tourists would even attempt to learn three or four words in Chinese. Other countries, particularly France, will hold you in contempt if you try to speak French. (Relax. They will hold you in contempt if you *don't* attempt French. They hold everybody, including native Francophones, in contempt.)
- Germans view an American attempting to speak German a little like a dog walking on its hind legs. They don't expect it to be done well, but the fact that it is done at all is amusing.
- You'll never be able to get it right. The German language is too complex. In fact, a major cause of German immigration to the United States in the 19th century was the promise of a better life, where one's children would never have to learn the subjunctive case in German.
- Even if your Oma still lives with you and refuses to speak anything but German to you (although she understands every word of *The Young and the Restless*), you still don't know German well enough. Grandmothers are notorious for speaking archaic dialects that are unintelligible to any and all born outside Oma's home valley.

- If you should somehow miraculously survive the pronunciation pitfalls and the dialect disasters, there are idioms. The German language is so literal that it actually becomes oddly poetic, or at least quirky. It unnerves Americans to have to ask for a hand-shoe (*Handschuh*) when what they want is a glove.
- Germans are blunt people: You'd expect them to spit out their verbs right away. But the Germans also have a sneaky sense of malice, so they hide their verbs at the end of their sentences or paragraphs or whatever. By the time the verb arrives, the average American has entirely forgotten the topic being discussed.

In very polite society, all the verbs are saved for the end of the evening when people are putting on their coats and being insincere about how much they enjoyed dinner. This need to allow the accumulated verbs to clear is why German etiquette requires that no new topics of conversation be brought up after coffee.

Do's and Don'ts of the German Language

- **Don't** learn how to ask "What does this cost?" or any other question that requires more than a yes or no answer. Germans will only *answer* you in German, talking faster than a hen on speed. What's worse, they mumble. You'll *never* understand.
- **Do** speak American-English. Drawl, even. It slows down your speech, which makes it easier for someone to decipher.
- **Do** speak softly and in a monotone. Stare straight at the person you're talking to and don't blink. This will make you seem vaguely threatening. Germans, like most Europeans, believe that all Americans are dangerous psychopaths.
- If you doubt this works, get on an elevator with someone *you* think is vaguely dangerous, and see how carefully you listen to everything he says.

- **Don't** speak with a British accent. Germans who can't speak a word of English know the class differences inherent in British accents. Americans, on the other hand, think anyone with *any* British accent is a close personal friend of Chuck and Di.

  Germans may not be crazy about Americans, but they *really* despise the British. While America has littered the European landscape with McDonald's and Coca-Cola signs, at least we don't send our football fans around the continent to trash other people's athletic stadiums.

- **Don't** swear under your breath. Often this will be the only English a German understands perfectly (after all, they've had GI's living in their country for more than 40 years), and you'll get the iciest stare you've ever seen.

- **Do** learn these phrases. They're the only useful ones you'll need:

  "Give me that..." (Wave your money when you say this, or you'll find out more than necessary about felony theft charges.)

  "Show me where the toilet is right now!" (You never ask for a "bathroom" no matter how much you may want to clean up after visiting some foreign toilets.)

  "Bring me some of whatever that man is eating." (With your command of foreign languages, you might end up eating something that's still squirming.)

  "Yes." (Not only is confession good for the soul, but you can get out of a lot of trouble by smiling like an idiot and agreeing to everything that's said.)

  "No." (Smile when you say this too, stranger.)

  "Thank you." (Just keep smiling and back slowly toward the door.)

  "Good-bye." (Use instead of "Hello" when you meet someone. People often will give you your way when they feel sorry for you because you're such an idiot.)

  "Hello." (Why bother being polite? You're never going to see these people again anyway.)

With a Name Like Himmelfreundpointner...

The old advertising slogan "With a name like Smuckers, it's got to be good" has always baffled me. Do they think that's a difficult name? Or is this their way of pointing out that this jam is made by Old World marmalade meisters? If you know what's good for you, you'll buy a lot, because they know you still have relatives in the old country, no?

Granted, most Americans have trouble pronouncing any name beyond Smith or Jones, but then a whole lot of Americans have trouble with Smith or Jones, particularly if it's in written form. But in my hometown there was no such thing as a Smith.

When I was in college, I dated a fine young woman from Michigan by the name of Smith. During school breaks and other extended separations, I would call her in Michigan, person-to-person, to avoid having to pay good money to talk to her horrible brother.

The operator in my town would come on the line, and I would give her the number and ask to speak with Margaret Smith. S-M-I-T-H, I would spell; *SMITH*, hissing like a lisping snake.

As soon as the phone was answered, the operator would announce, "Person-to-person call for Margaret Schmidt..." Margaret had already had some experiences with New Ulm, so she knew what to expect, but her parents didn't. The first time her father answered, and good and gentle soul that he was, he simply said, "I'm so sorry, but there's nobody here by that name," and hung up.

For all the Smiths and Jones of this country, I'd like to offer a listing of what *real* names look and sound like. These are names taken directly from the Berlin and Munich phone books, so they've *got* to be German.

ACTION NAMES

Blinker (and
 Winkelmann)
Gagg
Gschmack
Haack
Hitz
Humer
Jester
Kral
Popp
Rolloff
Scharmer
Schave
Scheer

Scheerer
Scheerz
Schield
Schissel
Schissler
Schitting
Schlepp
Schley
Schleyer
Schlipp
Schlitt
Schlitz
Schnapp
Schnese

Schnickel
Schnirring
Schnock
Schnorr
Schnoor (past tense of
 Schnorr)
Schock
Schoot
Schrunk
Schwinghammer
Sexauer
Wilfahrt
Zettel
Zink

NAMES THAT SOUND LIKE SOMETHING ELSE

Betz
Bippi
Bussmann
Boock
Butlar
Epple
Flick
Flor
Funk
Furbish
Geers
Geese
Heck
Koke

Pfaender
Pfuel
Schair
Scheff
Scherbel (a good pet
 for children)
Scherman (if you
 weren't Scherman,
 you wouldn't have a
 name like that)
Schik
Schild
Schill
Schleeve

Schmoker (desperately
 seeking a
 Schmoking
 schection)
Schoonover (I should
 hope so)
Schopp
Schoppe (an Olde
 English version of
 the above,
 presumably)
Sturm
Zaufl (opposite of
 Z'Wonderful)

BEER NAMES

Bierbauer
Bierfreund
Biermann
Bierwerth

Gutmann
Schmaltz
Schnack
Schnortz

Sittenauer
Tanke
Unterfahrt
Weinsheimer

POSITIVE NAMES

Bigi
Blessing
Bliss

Funke
Klier
Pfab

Weiss
Weiser
Weisenborn

NAMES THAT SOUND LIKE
YOU GOT STUCK WITH THEM

Bangert
Bigott
Bittruf
Blind
Bugge
Butzbach
Crone
Fink
Fohl
Fuhrhans
Gleek
Grumpe
Grunt

Junkereit
Klück
Krook
Moan
Nix
Nott
Pfanni
Pfau
Pflüb
Pfob
Plut
Sauer

Scheevel (who knows
what Scheevel lurks
in the hearts of men:
The Schadow proba-
bly does)
Schlib
Schmuck
Zotz
Zull

CONTRASTING NAMES

Schallow — Diepolder
Blessing — Heck
Schwahn — Schwein

Zeller — Beier
Faast — Schloe
Bigi — Schmahl

MORE NAMES

Bletschacher
Buttermilch
Butzhammer
Butzlaff
Eggensdorfer
Etzelsberger
Funckenhauser
Funnekötter
Geiselbrechtinger
Gstattenbauer
Gumpolteberger
Heimerdinger
Himmelfreundpointner
Himmelsdorfer
Kleinschnittzer
Kupferschmidt
Laudenschlaeger
Pfaffenberger
Pflaumbaum
Pfützenreuter
Schatschneider
Schildwachter

Schimmelpfennig
Schindeldecker
Schipplick
Schladweiler
Schlagenhaufer
Schlangenstein
Schleggelmilch
Schlichenmeyer
Schlook
Schlossmacher
Schmalzbauer
Schmeckpeper
Schmidberger
Schnakenberg
Schnarrenberger
Schneewind
Schneppmueller
Schnurbusch
Schobkegel
Schoechenmaier
Schoephoerster
Schreckenhaust

Schrettenbrunner
Schuffenhauer
Schultzetenberg
Sitzberger
Unsöld
Unterbuchberger
Unteregelsbacher
Untergangschnigg
Unterguttenberger
Unterpointer
Unterreithmaier
Unterumsberger
Unterhaslberger
Weidenschlagen
Wunderbaldinger
Zisselsberger
Zugschwert
Zusamenschneider
Zwickelbauer
Zwickenpflug

Updating the German Language

Americans have always had a horrible time learning other folks' languages, because we live in a quasi-literate culture full of people who think that "Verbs" is a video game.

Language teachers insist on teaching languages via grammatical forms most of us can't identify. I always assumed that the ablative dealt with ritual washings, while the genitive case was a nice way of saying venereal disease and probably was something you caught from the conjunctive.

There really *is* a pluperfect form. It "expresses action completed before a given or implied past time." After 15 minutes of rereading that description, I decided (after an implied time) that the only time I use the pluperfect form is halfway through a left-hand turn at a busy intersection, when I tell my terrified wife, "Oh, I could have *sworn* I turned on the blinkers...." Then she gives me pluperfect hell as we dodge the rusty Camaro with the quasi-obscene bumper sticker.

I've studied the German language for years, but I've also studied the weather for years, and I can't control either one. While the German language is a masterful instrument for discussing philosophical and theological concepts such as transfiguration, transcendence and transference, train schedules are all I can deal with given my limited vocabulary. The only theological impulse I've ever had in any German class was to beg God to keep the teacher from calling on me.

So I believe that the German language could stand some updating. I've given this a lot of thought and decided that my system isn't any more complicated than the system Herr Brakas and Herr Werner tried to teach me. But most important, my system conforms to the daily experience of German/Americans, so at least we know what we're talking about.

New Cases for General Usage

THE FUTURE COMPOSITE

Combining what you know you *ought* to do with what you know you *will* do.

EXAMPLE: "I'm going to start a *serious* diet on Monday."

THE INTERRUPTIVE

The Interruptive, or the Hypochondriacal, can be used to put an end to any discussion by topping whatever achievement, pain or insight is offered by someone else.

EXAMPLE: "I know just how you feel! My doctor said he had never seen a worse case of the flu than mine last year!"

THE PROPER SUBSTANTIVE

The so-called "bragging case." Used to brag about how important and prosperous you have become.

EXAMPLE: "When the writer from *Money* magazine called to do the article on young fast-trackers, I had to tell him I'd call him back tomorrow."

THE QUERULATIVE

Used by lawyers, confrontational talk-show hosts, the right wing and others whose main purpose in life is to argue.

EXAMPLE: "Well, that's *your* opinion, but any idiot can see that...."

TENDONITIOUS EXPECTORANT

Ever known you don't have a leg to stand on, but still been so mad you're ready to spit? Then you've already used the Tendonitious Expectorant without knowing it.

EXAMPLE: "Ja, well, you liberals! It's like, you know it's all tax and spend....You've never met a payroll, ja, that's it — you've never had to meet a payroll!"

Socializing Syntax

Often improperly called "The Dating Tenses," as if anything could be tenser than dating itself. Granted, most people assume such unnaturally good behavior on dates that the only thing you have to interpret is their grammar and the percentage of polyester in their wardrobe.

A good rule of thumb here is that anyone who describes himself or herself as "open to new experiences" but doesn't know that pasta is just spaghetti, only flatter, needs someone else as a mentor. You have enough problems without taking on remedial tutoring.

THE CONJUNCTORANT

Used when two or more things are to be joined, assuming everything goes well.

EXAMPLE: "Hey, baby, what's your sign?"

PRESENT PIXILATED

For most people, a transient form, used during the 20 or so minutes between falling in love (or getting an answer to your singles ad) and the onset of reality. However, if you're a person who likes the sort of "love taps" that require medical attention, you will use this form for years or the rest of your life, whichever comes first.

EXAMPLE: "This is going to be the real thing! He just moved back in with his mother after his divorce to save money."

THE PAST IMPROBABLE

If hindsight was such a great idea, your eye sockets would be on the same side of your body as your buns. But that doesn't stop some people from developing romances, governmental policies and family plans based on the view over their buns.

EXAMPLE: "If I had had a decent car back then, Karla would never have dumped me for that snotty pre-med student."

Special Use Cases:
The Jungenspracht Family of Cases

The Jungenspracht (like the Jungenstyl) is a linguistic family of cases favored by the young, who think that screaming "Why? ...Because! ...Why? ...Because!..." at each other for 20 minutes constitutes a conversation.

Actually a subtly nuanced form of communication, the Jungenspracht makes up in threats what it lacks in vocabulary and subtlety.

FEMININE FUTURE ABSOLUTE CONDITIONAL

Commonly used by older sisters to affect future behavior with unspecified threats.

EXAMPLE: "If my diary isn't back on my desk in 15 minutes, I will tell every one of your friends what you say in your sleep."

THE NONCAUSAL HYSTERICAL

The so-called "What Cause? What Effect?" clause favored by younger siblings, usually just before disaster strikes.

EXAMPLE: "I was just standing there, minding my own business, Xeroxing my sister's diary, when she totally freaked out for no reason at all!"

TRANSITIONAL FUTURE MASCULINE IMPERATIVE

Favored by bigger brothers to explain the consequences of continuing with your present behavior.

EXAMPLE: "If you don't give me your sandwich before I count to 10, I'm going to lock you in the hog pen...."

Swearing for German/Americans

Considering how blunt-spoken German/Americans are in most matters, we still have an incredible number of verbal taboos.

We act as if words themselves have magical powers. Speak of the devil, and he appears. We know sex education is bad because if we *say* something, kids magically will be impelled to *do* it. We dress up that little superstition by calling it "putting ideas into kids' heads," as if teenage sexuality was something that needed to be jump-started by a grown-up.

To avoid speaking of the devil, we have devised an elaborate system of euphemisms, which refer to everything and mean nothing. "That" is our favorite. "That" refers to body parts, acts, excretions, certain kinds of people and whole anatomical areas.

"It" is even more delicate and prissy than "that," because "it" is even less specific, if that's possible. "That way" is another good denunciation dependent on voice tone for meaning. Someone who is "that way" is possibly pregnant, perpetually horny, gay or all of the above.

So how can you discuss humanity's favorite pastime without offending German/American sensibilities? Practice these phrases. Soon you too will know the nasty thrill of saying a naughty word in such a way that not even your relatives can criticize you for bad language.

Always curl your lip when you let these terms slip out. If necessary, rub your upper gums with tabasco sauce. Remember, it's not the thought, word or even the *deed* that you're judging. You're judging the *person*!

Permissible German/American Euphemisms for Sex

That...
It...
Doing it...
Er, you know...
Acting like a married couple...
Taking their honeymoon before they take their vows...
Took advantage...
Got her in a family way...
PG...
Shacking up...

Permissible German/American Euphemisms for Body Parts

It...
That...
That thing...
Those things...
You know...
His...
Her...
Down there...

Permissible German/American Cussing

Considering how much craziness there is in the world, anyone who hasn't needed to cuss his or her lungs out now and then simply hasn't been paying attention.

German/Americans are particularly fond of a couple of cusses that only barely mask the rage behind them:

"So-called" — Our favorite slander, it means "S. O. B.," as in "that *so-called* liberal...."

"Kookie," "way out" or **"far out"** — Anyone who uses this phrase thinks:

1. It's the ultimate in sarcasm;
2. It's a stinging rebuke;
3. It's how hippies and beatniks talk; and
4. The world is still overrun by hordes of hippies and beatniks.

These terms refer to anything a very sheltered person in a very small town thinks is new, unexpected or out-of-the-ordinary. Movies without happy endings, nonrepresentational art, liberal politics and newcomers who have moved to town less than 15 years ago are all blanketed by this condemnation.

High-Context Innuendo

German/Americans live in what is called a "high-context society." That means we already know everything there is to know about each other. We know and we disapprove.

You can cuss in a high-context society by innuendo alone. Try it! When you're with a friend, just say "He's... you know...." If you wag your hand back and forth, your friend probably thinks he's lazy. Put your hand out, palm down, fingers extended, rocking like the deck of a troubled ship, and you suggest that he's crazy.

Shrug your shoulders, and you're suggesting that he seduced your daughter and then changed his telephone number. Curl your lip, and you hint that he's not a German/American.

Of course, things like this can backfire, and your friend might go spreading the word that your dumb daughter got herself mixed up with a lazy, crazy Swede.

ALL the ANSWERS

by Ann Hofmeister, Ph.D.

LEARN HOW TO:

Treat Children Like Legally Liable Adults! Treat Adults Like Incompetent Children!

TIRED of annoying discussions and the so-called free exchange of ideas? **SICK** of backtalk, dissent and openness? **BORED** with "far out" opinions, unverifiable assertions and people who "share" their "experiences and observations"? **STOP** all this idle chatter with ANSWERS like these:

"You'd be better off if you just stopped whining!"

"What the artist (writer/director/choreographer/etc.) meant was . . ."

"God has told me that he wants *you* to . . ."

"With your weight problem, you shouldn't even *consider* buying a whirlpool! You know how dangerous they are for your heart!"

"You don't *really* expect me to believe that, do you?"

"No wonder they didn't hire you. Look how you're dressed!"

"You're going to get ice under your shingles and water into your attic because you didn't clean out your gutters last fall!"

"You have nobody but yourself to blame!"

SPECIAL INTRODUCTION BY MORTON DOWNEY, JR.!

Doing Things the Right Way

There is an equation you should know. One German/ American equals a certainty. Two German/Americans equal an argument. Four German/Americans equal a religion and eight German/Americans equal two religions at each other's throat.

This is because German/Americans know there is a right way and a wrong way to do everything. Our way and your way. But because we don't always see eye-to-eye even with each other, the issue is usually one of my way and your way.

Furthermore, my way is the right way right up to the moment I decide to do it differently. What makes it exciting for everybody is that we give neither warnings nor explanations. We just get up one morning and there's a new right way.

Heaven help the colleague, customer or friend who still thinks the old way is the right way and tries to remind us of how we used to do things. We make these little mid-course corrections because we know that it's good for everyone to keep on their toes. Only table salt has done more than this policy to keep German/Americans' blood pressure in triple digits.

German/Americans believe that our hyper-rationality makes us somehow special. We see ourselves as Mr. Spock with blond eyebrows. The problem with convincing yourself that *your* habits are deeply rooted in logic is that other people with different habits are then by definition illogical people. And everybody knows that illogical people are not to be taken seriously.

Because we are absolutely right, there's no need for discussion. We'll just give a couple of examples and let you compare and contrast. Then just do whatever we do, and watch the backtalk.

German Engineering Standards

Germans like to suggest that they are somehow responsible for every useful invention. If they didn't invent it outright, they wrote the operating manual.

Americans don't like this sort of attitude. We're suspicious of anyone who works hard, is tremendously disciplined and creates a superior product. This is why the only automotive innovation the United States has developed in the past 30 years is the radar detector.

A PRODUCT-BY-PRODUCT COMPARISON

GERMANY:	UNITED STATES:
AUTOMOBILE INNOVATIONS	
Cars with the muscle under a suit coat	Muscle cars that embarrass anyone born north of the Mason/Dixon line
Cars that travel safely at high speeds	Radar detectors
POP ICONOGRAPHY	
Antique religious carvings	Whiskey bottles that look like Elvis Presley
Marzipan pigs	Unicorn tapestries, velvet paintings
CHRISTMAS COOKIES	
Lebkuchen, Stollen & Springerle	Sugar cookies with sprinkles
BEER	
More than a thousand brands of *real* beer	Lite beer
Rheinwein, Liebfraumilch	Wine coolers
DESSERTS	
Black Forest torte	Sara Lee frozen chocolate cake

What Does the United States Do Better Than Germany?

I'm as patriotic as the next fellow. Heck, I even say the Pledge of Allegiance every morning before I have my breakfast cereal. As a true patriot, I'd like to point out some of the triumphs of contemporary American corporate life. These are things we do better than anyone in the world, even the Germans. We may not deliver them as fast, nor will they last as long, but they're *our* contribution to the archeological record.

AMERICA'S #1 IN:

SODA POP — Sometimes it seems like all of America's creativity went into soda pop. We have umpteen versions of the old brown fizzie so you can get no caffeine or ultra-caffeine, no-calorie or ultra-calorie, no salt, no preservatives, no chemicals and even a soda-pop-free all natural juice soft drink.

If Detroit had as much energy and pizzazz as the soft drink people, they'd be driving Chevys on "Miami Vice."

STORE HOURS — The quality of the merchandise may be abysmal, but you can almost *always* go shopping in the United States! We have convenience stores whose only door locks are on the toilets.

PARKING SPOTS — German streets are so narrow you have to park half on the sidewalk. Of course, Germany also has effective, efficient public transportation, so you don't *need* to park. In the United States you can park anywhere! Assuming it isn't a snow emergency or your meter isn't expired.

CORPORATE PUBLIC RELATIONS — Germans have this arrogant attitude: "If you build it right the first time, you won't have to run around being nice when you fix it."

The United States has the biggest public-relations industry in the world, and it's not hard to figure out why.

POPULAR MOVIES — Miss a first-run movie here and hate to watch the VCR? Take a vacation in Europe and catch all of last year's American flicks. Or go back home and catch the three-year-old European movies at the University Film Society, if you're lucky.

POP MUSIC — The average German record has a 50-year-old chamber of commerce dude on the cover and is titled "Wolfgang Zweidelmacher and the Tyrolean All-Stars Play Johann Strauss's Greatest Hits." Not exactly the sort of record that Jerry Falwell plays backwards to uncover Satanic messages.

TV COMMERCIALS — Critics of overproduced American commercials should note that "rustic" commercials (i.e., those with poor production values) are neither more honest nor less manipulative. They're just clumsier, sort of like the public service announcements American stations run at 3 a.m.

Right and Wrong in Peanut-Butter Sandwiches

Right and wrong are distinctions too important to save for profound issues like: "Should I sell hammers to the Pentagon for $1,000 each, and if not, why not?"

Not many of us are lucky enough to have the Pentagon open a charge account with us, so we never get to face such dilemmas. But we German/Americans do know that everything in life is either right or wrong. We further know that it is our job to make that distinction clear to those who appear uncertain.

We know that nothing in life is too trivial to be wrong. Where you squeeze the toothpaste tube, for example. The right way to do it is the scientific way: at the far end, conserving energy and time. Only irrational people grab the tube sloppily, thus wasting time, energy and expensive toothpaste!

Similarly, there are right and wrong ways to make peanut-butter sandwiches. Follow the illustrations below and you will be secure in the knowledge that you are doing everything right!

THE RIGHT WAY:

Remove slices from loaf and lay them open as you would a book.

Place slices side by side. Close slices as you would close a book.

Slices match contours perfectly.

THE WRONG WAY:

Don't pay any attention to how you're taking bread out. Put it anywhere on the board. See if I care.

Just *try* to close this up.

Slices are reversed, and the whole sandwich is *ruined* because the tough bottom crust is now in two places.

ABSOLUTE WORST WAY:

It's only going to make it worse if you eat off the crusts all around the sandwich!

Trying to make amends by turning the slices around as you should have in the first place is futile.

In fact, it's counterproductive, and you've just managed to make things twice as bad!

Outsmarting the Trendsetters.

They tell me that yuppiedom has been replaced by a kinder, gentler nation, but it's hard to see from where I sit. I'll believe it when I see Tom Wolfe in a bowling league.

It takes new fashions some time to percolate into German/American communities. As far as I can tell, some folks around here still are wallowing their way through an acquisitive stage that would do Nancy Reagan proud. So you still need to know how to deal with those inflicted with designeritis, the delusion that a signature on your jeans will make your butt look thinner.

How do good, no-money-down, no-money-spent German/Americans cope with forced social contact with yups? We dig in our heels and revert to type. We believe that the mark of a person isn't how much money he or she makes, it's how much they've *saved*! And you sure aren't going to be saving much squandering your paycheck on espresso machines.

We should be proud of our careful ways. German/Americans are the country's leading source of Depression glass. Of course, we have to wash the breakfast eggs off the plates before we sell them, because we're still using them. If Melmac ever becomes a collector's item, it will make even more old German/Americans rich than when prices for farmland went through the ceiling.

The important thing to remember about today's new gadgets and pretensions is that they all have equivalents within your own life. In other words, you probably already have what some yup is desperate to acquire, and you haven't been overcharged for it.

Allow me to present a chart comparing the object of yuppie desire with the reality in your own life. Both columns are absolutely equal in function. Not only is your column cheaper, but you can be a reverse-snob!

YUPPIE CONVERSION CHART
of
ABSOLUTE EQUIVALENCES

YUPPIE GOAL	GERMAN/AMERICAN REALITY
Cuisinart from the Sharper Image	Slicer-dicer from the state fair
Chilled quail and pasta salad	Macaroni salad with cocktail wieners
Snacking on cold pasta	Stuffing your face with leftover spaghetti
Lobster salad	Tuna salad
Très bien, salut!	Three-bean salad
Croissants	Wonder Bread
Potage des champignons	Campbell's Cream of Mushroom Soup
Pâté	Braunschweiger
Wine and cheese tastings	Cheetos and Hauenstein at half-time
Perrier	Alka-Seltzer
Glacéed Fruits	Strawberries in Jell-O
Béarnaise sauce	White gravy

LOCAL WOMAN WINS PRESTIGIOUS ART COMPETITION

Karla Krankenschwester today won the 23rd annual Greater Cleveland Hummel Look-alike Contest, adult division, for her portrayal of "The Umbrella Girl, Hummel Listing #152-B," pictured above.

The Greater Cleveland Hummel Look-alike Contest is a prestigious competition in the world of collectibles, and winning it often leads to a modeling career working for pattern companies and fabric stores.

Contestants are judged on four criteria:

1. Thickness of clothing: The use of industrial-strength batting in Mrs. Krankenschwester's costume helped to match the ceramic proportions of the original artwork's costume.

2. Adorability: Mrs. Krankenschwester was judged to have "perfectly embodied the helpless female so foreign to German/American reality, yet so dear to our hearts as a concept," as one smitten judge so aptly put it.

3. Improbability of pose: Reality is for the MacNeil/Lehrer Newshour, not Hummel figurines. The judges ruled that sitting on the wet ground in the middle of a rainstorm holding a metal umbrella would be considered perfectly realistic in the happy world of collectibles.

4. Authenticity: Mrs. Krankenschwester's painted eyebrows, moussed wig and painted coat were admirable, but her winning edge was provided by her consummate attention to detail.

As every collector knows, the age of a Hummel figurine can be determined by the style of the trademark on the figurine's base. Born in 1948, Mrs. Krankenschwester had the 1948 version of the Hummel Bee tattooed on *her* base. "I got the idea from former Secretary of State George Schultz, who has the Princeton Tiger tattooed on his, er…, base too," claims the politically aware Mrs. Krankenschwester.

Kitsch and Other Cultural Contributions

Some people see the world and say *why me*? German/ Americans see the world and say *why not*! That's where most of the trouble starts. Actually, our usual response to the world is, "Oh, crapola." So we establish our own little world that eliminates the crapola. *Our* little world. Where everybody does things *our* way. Perfect. Tidy. Sentimental.

In Germany, this sense of sentimental control manifests itself in snow shakers. A snow shaker contains a perfect little world under glass that you can grab and shake up, just to watch things fly through the air. *Sehr Deutsch*.

Germans and German/Americans are united in their love of Hummel figurines, pricey little porcelains that feature children's bodies and strangely adult heads, including plucked eyebrows, painted lips and mascaraed eyelashes. Just the sort of composite child/woman some radical feminists have been warning against.

Dolls have a particular fascination for German/Americans, because dolls never talk back no matter how we dress or treat them. Stick Barbie and Ken in a Lady of Spain doll tableau and they'll stay there for years, never once complaining that their backs ache or yapping about how much they hate flamenco costumes.

Connoisseurs would call this tableau kitsch. But they also think performance art is high art, even though performance art is usually nothing more than dressing up dolls and making them stand around in awkward poses.

German/Americans realize that the art/kitsch debate is hollow because we know that one generation's kitsch is the next generation's folk art. So the next time you see a paint-by-number velvet-painting kit, don't think kitsch. Think *heirloom*!

German Opera:
Food for the Soul, Work for the Mind

Opera is very important to German/Americans, for reasons none of their children can understand. Germany practically invented music. If it were not for Bach, Beethoven, Wagner, Brahms, Handel, Schumann and others, concert halls would be warehouses for snowmobile parts.

Unfortunately, there is good opera, and there is bad opera. German opera and Italian opera. German opera requires Cliffs Notes to fully understand the plot. On the other hand, in an Italian opera, you don't *want* to understand what they're up to. If you insist on knowing what's going on, just pick up a copy of *Soap Opera Digest* at the supermarket.

By way of explanation, allow me to outline two operas. "La Ninni di Belladonna," one of the best loved works by Italy's most realistic operatist, Giacomo Punchinella (1812-1896). Compare this to "Die Grossische Kopf Schmerz," by Wulfgang Schnarlmann (1844-1902). Only Schnarlmann's untimely nervous breakdown kept him from inflicting even more insight onto the world.

"La Ninni di Belladonna"
An Operatic Diversion

The Cannelloni clan has gathered to celebrate the Feast of the Hysterical Virgins, a quaint and colorful ceremony in San Penitente di Whacko, the ancient seat of the Cannelloni clan. The Cannelloni are a proud family, tracing their lineage all the way back to the infamous Duke of Cellulite in the 12th century.

Today, the Parade of the Hysterical Virgins will be led for the last time by Donna Obsequious, who is to be betrothed to the cruel Don Ameche. Although his formal title would be Don Don Ameche, the cruel Don Don recently stabbed his brother Don Billy Bob when Billy Bob called him Don Don in a public place.

Donna Obsequious doesn't want to marry the aged and cruel Don Don Ameche, but she knows she must, for otherwise all her great tragic arias won't make any sense at all. She is secretly in love with Don Johnsono and wants to run away with him to Miami.

Forced to surrender to her father's wishes, Donna Obsequious reluctantly marries the aged and cruel Don Ameche in a pompous and endless wedding ceremony that chews up most of the second act.

Within a month, and shortly after the intermission, Donna Obsequious and Don Johnsono just happen to be in the quaint and colorful market of San Penitente. Their eyes meet, and they exchange meaningful glances. Her glances tell of her great sadness, of remorse, of the pain of young love denied. His glances tell of some bad sausage he ate yesterday.

Lurking in the shadows of the quaint and colorful market is Zucchini, a seller of clinically unproven cancer cures. She sees the young lovers batting their eyes at each other across the entire width of the stage. Hoping to make a few bucks off this, she hurries to the aged and cruel Don Ameche to deliver her famous recitative, "I didn't want to tell you, but I thought you should know..."

Without checking her facts, Don Don swings into his famous "Laughing Revenge" aria, where he sings "Ah-ha-ha-ha" (or perhaps, "Ah-hack-hack-hack," for he is a heavy smoker), "Ah-ha-ha-ha, another man has looked at her, and therefore to protect my honor, I must kill her, and her kinsmen, and her kinswomen, and her kinspoodle. Ah-ha-ha-ha, how wretched am I. Poor me, look what she made me do."

Perhaps in 19th-century Italy, this was considered a normal romantic relationship. But in Minnesota today, this dude would be under court-appointed psychiatric care.

Rushing through the quaint and colorful marketplace, full of quaint and cowering peasants, the aged and cruel D.D.A. meets Donna Obsequious, who inexplicably is carrying a basket of well-cooked sausage. Enraged, he plunges a knife into her heart. This wound is so seriously fatal that she can sing only another 20 minutes or so.

She tells Don Don that she really *does* love him, sort of, kind of, you know, but was on her way to the convent where she could become a public-health nursing nun, specializing in food-poisoning cases. Then she dies, and he sings a bunch more, and then Don Johnsono comes on and sings a bunch of stuff, and one of them stabs the other, and then everybody in the audience jumps up and claps hysterically.

Even though the only word in Italian most of the audience knows is *ristorante*, they all instinctively know the difference between *brava* and *bravo*. On the way out of the opera house, the men all swagger and try to flirt with the women, but the women are all enjoying a good little cry and could care less what those old roosters want.

"Die Grossische Kopf Schmerz"
An Immense Operatic and Philosophic Masterpiece in One Endless Act

As the house lights dim, there is a rustle of paper as the audience puts away the libretti and scores they have been studying to familiarize themselves with the theories to be propounded tonight. German audiences do *not* like to be surprised.

After a long prelude of low, ominous notes symbolizing the beginnings of the universe and the awakening of human consciousness after the breakdown of bicameral neurological functioning, Jedermann (Everyman) is seen wandering alone on a stage cluttered with the flotsam and jetsam of consumer society.

After the audience has had an opportunity to assimilate the meaning of the setting and the meaninglessness of lives lived without a greater purpose, Jedermann breaks his angry silence.

In a voice only slightly softer than a heavy-metal concert, he sings touchingly of the glories of nature; of the beauty of the sunrise amid the purity of the mountains; and of the vastness of the universe as imaged by multiple-dish radio telescopes.

Then Erde (the Goddess Earth) materializes as a hologram and sings for what seems like forever about how Jedermann's lust for dominance and power is ruining his life, souring his inter-personal relationships, and generally mucking up the world with physical, psychic and chemical pollution.

To symbolize the destruction, she hands him a withered rose and a dead eel, then demands that he make a large contribution to the Green Party. He stiffs her on the contribution but agrees to sign a petition condemning the handling of the Chernobyl affair.

By now they have been singing for more than three hours, each bringing in expert witnesses to testify on their behalf. Erde has become increasingly weak during the last half-hour, in part because Jedermann has been sitting on her chest to symbolize all kinds of stuff.

The opera ends when the music swells and Jedermann sweeps up to his house with the new security system. In tones that ring with finality, he announces as the curtain falls that he is going to get an unlisted telephone number.

The audience immediately breaks into small discussion groups to analyze the evening. Blue test booklets are passed out immediately, and anyone who can quote all of Nietzsche's basic theorems in German is allowed to test out and go home early.

Schadenfreude:
Semi-innocent Delights

The Germans have given us many wonderful words, most of them at least six feet long. They are remarkably precise words that mean things like "The-Union-and-Collective-Bargaining-Agent-of-the-Boiler-Makers,-Electricians,-Carpenters,-Sea-Worthiness-Inspectors,-Sailors,-First-Mates-River-Boat-Captains-of-Rhine-River-Tugboats,-Barges,-Ferries,-Touring-Craft-and-Dirigible-Operators-Association." All in one word.

What's worse, given the formality of the Germans, anyone attempting to negotiate with that union couldn't just call it "the union." They'd have to use that whole paragraph/word, even when they only meant "youse guys."

Luckily, the Germans also have given us words that are just as precise but a whole lot shorter. They may have started out longer, but they've been rubbed smooth by constant use.

One word that gets daily use is *Schadenfreude*. It means the secret delight we all take at the misfortunes of others. Particularly when the others are bullies, pompous asses or well-placed fools. Schadenfreude doesn't involve heavy-duty revenge. It's just a richly deserved comeuppance.

You can be sure that you're feeling *Schadenfreude* when your response to a tale of woe is to say, "*Das tut mir Leid!* — That breaks my heart!"

Schadenfreude in Daily Life

1. You are indulging yourself at the Häagen-Daz shop. Who should walk in but your old aerobics instructor, who inexplicably has developed a little weight problem of her own in the past couple of years. *Das tut mir Leid!*
2. You are 6 years old. Your older brother has been tormenting you all morning. Suddenly your mother discovers the lamp you broke. Despite his protests, she is convinced that he did it. You get to watch as he gets the spanking. *Das tut mir Leid!*
3. The rain has turned to sleet, and the streets are sheer ice. Everybody in town is driving about 20 miles per hour, when a Porsche with California plates and a Jazzercise bumper sticker weaves through traffic at 45. When you get to the bend in the road, the Porsche is augured into a huge snowbank. *Das tut mir Leid!*
4. You are a traffic cop. You have just pulled over a car for doing 50 in a 30-mile zone. Inside at the wheel is the credit manager who last week curtly refused your application for a Visa card. *Das tut mir Leid!*
5. You are working late at night in a convenience store. After 1 a.m. (the legal curfew for selling beer), the cop who maced your girlfriend at a peaceful protest shows up and demands you sell him beer. *Das tut mir Leid!*
6. The old grump with the bulging grocery cart who pushed ahead of you in the express lane is told by a rude teenage clerk to go somewhere else. *Das tut mir Leid!*

7. You work at a large city bank processing checks for local businesses. One Monday morning, you recognize the name of a prominent businessman and moralist from your hometown. His $50 check is furtively made out to cash. Stamped on the back, however, is "FiFi's Sauna & Rap Parlor." You happen to know that his wife balances the family checkbook. *Das tut mir Leid!*

8. The high school guidance counselor who told you that girls shouldn't even consider math as a college major loses her job to a marginally qualified male. *Das tut mir Leid!*

9. You have worked your butt off on an important college paper. The "Joe Cool" frat boy next to you has paid someone to retype a paper from his fraternity's "papers and tests" files. The professor recognizes the paper when it is handed in, and flunks the kid on the spot. *Das tut mir Leid!*

10. The man who started the "Loyalty and Patriotism" committee at the local veterans club has denounced your work with the Izaak Walton League as "Communist-inspired so-called environmentalism." In the paper one fine day, you read that he has not filed tax returns since 1976. *Das tut mir Leid!*

11. You are a farmer in the north woods. On your way to feed some cattle at a remote pasture, you come across two arrogant city boys hunting on your land. You ask them not to hunt there. They just wave their beer bottles at you. That evening, you have to go back to get them down from the tree where they had been chased by a bear. *Das tut mir Leid!*

12. A real estate developer from the city buys 70 acres of riverfront property with intentions of starting a housing tract called "River-Vue." Despite local advice and opposition, he bulldozes house sites and roads. When the river recovers from its drought levels, the local paper runs a photo of the development sign halfway underwater. *Das tut mir Leid!*

The Review Committee for the Renewal of Fishing Licenses has decided to put some teeth into the renewal process by publicly examining each applicant to determine his/her qualifications and preparation for participation. By establishing standards, the committee hopes to raise the status of sport fishing and possibly get a network TV contract for the Annual Fishing Opener, when the Minnesota Governor throws out the first fish of the season.

13. At your college reunion, you see your old flame and the man she dumped you to marry. Nowadays he is choleric, puffy and drinks a lot. She looks a little claustrophobic. *Das tut mir Leid!*

14. For the past two hours, you have been stuck going 47 miles per hour behind a motor home large enough to have its own zip code. Exhausted, you stop for lunch. As you are leaving, you recognize the motor home's owner walking to the gas station with a large gas can. *Das tut mir Leid!*

15. On your first date, he blathers on about his romantic exploits. After two and a half hours of uninterrupted details, he pauses long enough to ask you what you do

for a living. You tell him you are a vice officer, and he believes you. *Das tut mir Leid!*

16. The office vulgarian gets totally bombed at the office Christmas party and wins what his female colleagues refer to ever after as "The Triple Crown," when he manages to pinch or pat the fannies of the corporate legal counsel, the equal opportunities officer, and the Mormon wife of the new CEO. *Das tut mir Leid!*

Good Things the Germans Have Given Us

America is a rich melange of cultures. Each wave of immigrants has contributed to this cultural stew. Only on Main Street, U.S.A., can you find an Indian curry restaurant in the thankless business of introducing spicy food to Lutherans next to the Tai Kwon Do Martial Arts Emporium next to a music store catering to salsa and reggae musicians.

The English have given us great holidays, like St. Swithin's Day (St. Swithin, as you will recall, was the wise counselor to King Ethelred the Unready). The French have replaced Wonder Bread with croissants, now conveniently sold in gas stations so the eternally mobile yuppie can always have a supply of soft, tasteless, squishy bread.

The Italians have convinced us that restaurants ought to be decorated with red-flocked Con-tact paper. General Noriega of Panama did his best to lessen the dependency of America's youth on alcohol as their recreational drug of choice. And the Icelanders have given the piece of cod to America's dieters.

But what have the Germans given us, except, indirectly, some great Irving Berlin World War I songs like "Over There"? Or our entire space program? Or Arnold Schwarzenegger? Let me refresh your memory.

German Contributions to American Culture

Heinies —America's most versatile hairstyle: Daring in the late 1940s, de rigueur in the '50s, deadly dull in the '60s, and now delightfully feminine in the '80s.

Sauerkraut balls — The culinary equivalent of a hair ball for a cat, except we consider sauerkraut balls to be edible. Surprisingly, German/American hostesses often serve sauerkraut balls to guests whom the hostess *wants* to return.

Audi — A car so luxurious that it indeed *does* have a mind of its own. Unfortunately, that little mind might just be thinking about accelerating without telling you.

Lederhosen — Funny leather shorts for men with ugly knees. Some say their main function is to draw attention away from some truly Teutonic beer bellies.

Beer — The gift that America never got right. The phrase "good American beer" is something of an oxymoron, like "fine English cuisine" or "Swedish volatility."

Wieners — Frankfurters, bratwurst, hot dogs — call them what you will, they are the little mystery meats of American childhood. Without them, there would be no women in the American workplace, because every American mom would have to spend every waking moment cooking macrobiotic meals out of her holistic, health-grain cookbook.

Jerry cans and jerry-rigging (but not gerrymandering) — Jerry cans were those funny gas cans on the backs of Jeeps when we were kids. Jerry-rigging refers to Rube Goldberg techniques applied to the real world. Gerrymandering is a fine old American tradition. We didn't need some foreigner to teach us how to do *that!*

Things We *Should* Have Adopted from the Germans

Himbeere Torte — Along with Black Forest torte, Himbeere torte is the best theological proof that Adam and Eve were Germans. They *must* have smuggled these two out of Eden.

Gemütlichkeit —Some describe it as nirvana washed down by the best of the Bavarian beers. Others describe it as deep contentment, friendship and/or jolliness. It comes in many varieties and ought to be bottled and sprayed over the world's trouble spots.

Fasching — A *lot* of Lutherans have never fully forgiven Martin Luther for depriving us of this Germanic version of *Karneval*. Because rushing seminaked through the February streets of Rothenburg is inadvisable, Germans in the more Catholic south celebrate *Fasching* by buying books that provide page-long toasts and party speeches that must be memorized. This is as close as Germans get to spontaneity.

Things It's Just as Well We Left in Germany

Carp as a foodstuff — They jelly it, they boil it, they broil it, they bread it, and they smile when they eat it! They'll tell you that German carp is a finer critter than the common mud-sucking American carp, and if you believe that, you probably believe that the Maginot Line really *was* built to store grain.

Marzipan — Considered edible by the same people who think cotton candy is a taste treat, marzipan is an endlessly adaptive sculpting material. Germans use it to make everything from perfect replicas of other foodstuffs to statues of little piggies enjoying conjugal relations. If marzipan ever caught on in the United States, we would just use it to make little shrines to Elvis.

Rehabilitating the Pig

Pigs need to hire a good public relations agency, the kind made up of greedy former administration officials who specialize in making drug-running dictators look like our patriotic allies.

Pigs have a major image problem. I defy you to think of a positive phrase, image or idea involving pigs. Consider such stereotypes as sexist pigs with little piggy eyes who pig-out, who go hog-wild, hog the road or act like swine slopping at the trough. Every old boar knows you can't make a silk purse out of a sow's ear, and some swine are as lazy as a hog in a mud puddle.

German/Americans have contributed heavily to these unfortunate stereotypes, partly because we like our wurst, which means we've got to have a lot of pigs around to assure a steady supply of personal wursts. But despite, or perhaps because of, this experience with raising pigs, German/Americans also have become some of the best pig cursers in the country.

The greatest offense one kid could throw at another in the little German/American town I grew up in was to call someone a *Schweinhund*, a pig dog. The fact that none of us knew what it meant made it even dirtier.

Hog-bashing is hypocritical in a country as fond as we are of pork chops, hot dogs and sausages. We've got to knock off this business of attributing the most unpleasant aspects of humanity to the unoffending hog. If the animal-rights movement ever gets any real political power, pigs one day may be able to sue the human race for slander.

I think it's time we all sat down and ran through a little reality check about humans versus hogs.

PIG POSITIVES
Athletic Pigs

There *are* athletic pigs. In fact, one of the biggest attractions at many county fairs are the pig races.

It should be noted that the crowds at pig races have noticeably higher intelligence, better skin tones and healthier lifestyles than the crowds watching dog races, for instance.

- The only reason pigs race is for an immediate reward. The only reward they give a damn about is Oreo cookies.
- Pigs do not jog for "psychological" reasons. They have a sneaking suspicion that they are going to get eaten no matter how good they feel about themselves.
- No pig has ever been seen speed-walking in public.
- Athletic pigs do not take steroids, use caffeine suppositories as stimulants, or train under East German coaches. This is why there are no Porcine Olympics, and is the only thing that has saved us from the spectacle of sportscasters fawning over whoever wins these events.
- Pigs do not read magazine articles about their Body Mass Index, their percentage of body fat or expensive athletic paraphernalia.
- Since pigs do not bicycle, they do not wear black skin-tight bermuda shorts. They know they will be sausage soon enough.
- Athletic pigs do not do celebrity commercials, endorsing products which they have no qualifications to judge.
- Athletic pigs do not give speeches to high school athletic associations about "Sports as a Metaphor for Successful Living."
- Athletic pigs do not do anti-drug commercials when they are too stoned to talk.

Political Pigs

Pigs have a distinctly political side. Instead of dissecting piglets in biology class, schoolchildren ought to be observing live pigs to learn about human behavior.

The most dramatic lesson in political science I ever got came from watching a pen full of pigs go into a blood frenzy when a snake tried to make a shortcut across their pen. I was only 7 years old, but I immediately understood mass movements.

- Pigs are more curious than humans. When a pig wants to know about something, it breaks down the fence. It does not appoint a congressional fact-finding committee whose job it is to stick the opposition with the blame for the situation, obfuscate the reality of the problem, and guard against any future resolution of the issue.
- Like most politicians, pigs have no sense of irony. They almost never laugh when confronted with phrases like "military intelligence," "read my lips," "the trickle-down theory" or the notion of calling *our* terrorists "Freedom Fighters."
- Some researchers say that pigs may be among the very few who actually believe in the validity of such ideas.
- Pigs are ambiguously intelligent animals. They are clever enough to be easily trained by a kid in 4-H, but stupid enough that they never guess that the kid they love and trust eventually will kill and eat them. Since politics doesn't require much more intellect than this, one can only assume that pigs shun politics because of their contempt for political action committees.
- Far fewer pigs than humans believe that the Contras are "the moral equivalent of the Founding Fathers."

Social Pigs

Pigs are very social animals. They cuddle together even if they're not trying to stay warm, and they are affectionate even when they're not looking for sex. I personally know of several marriages that could have been saved by less effort.

Pigs are ambiguously intelligent but very affectionate.

- While it is true that pigs do have "piggy little eyes" and big snouts, who among us can honestly say they haven't dated worse? And if truth be known, unless you met that date in a piano bar singing along with "Feelings," it probably wasn't all that awful.

- Many people consider pigs unclean and therefore refuse to eat them. They think this hurts pigs' feelings. It does not.

  Pigs realize this unclean business is sort of circular. If people were serious about eating only those animals with a fetish for cleaning themselves, there would be vast herds of kitty cats grazing the plains of Wyoming.

- "Pigging out" is a human feeding notion. Pigs are *supposed* to gain massive amounts of weight. It's on their Management by Objective list. Of course, when they achieve their MBO goals, somebody eats them.

Cultural Pigs

Pigs are not responsible in any way for:

- Morton Downey Jr. and his guests.
- Geraldo Rivera or supermarket tabloids.
- Madonna, Sean Penn or the Brat Pack.
- Jimmy Swaggart, Jim and Tammy Faye Bakker or Oral Roberts.
- Impeached Governor Evan Meacham, Pat Robertson, David Duke, skinheads or the white rights movement.
- The TV heirs of "Queen for a Day," where the wretched of the earth exhibit their moral deformities in exchange for our sympathy: shows like Sally Jessie Raphael, and, increasingly, Oprah Winfrey and Donahue.
- "High-concept" movies. "High-concept" means an entire plot line that can be described in a single low-brow sentence.
- The embarrassing public pronouncements of Tama Janowitz, Norman Mailer or Dr. Joyce Brothers.
- Cultural heros such as Ivana and Donald Trump, Ivan Boesky, Pia Zadora, Frank Lorenzo, the Helmsleys, or anyone associated with a Leveraged Buyout of any corporation.

Hoarding and Counting as a Hobby

A hobby is a way of expressing your life's values in tangible form. Not surprisingly, German/American hobbies tend to be precise, verifiable and encyclopedic. In other words, hobbies that are fussy and judgmental.

Making scale models of military equipment is a great German/American hobby. Building the model is a precision process, and painting it allows for the exhaustive, totally useless scholarship so beloved by hobbyists.

For the purist, it's not enough simply to make a 1:35 scale model of a Sherman tank. You've got to study production records of the war plant that manufactured Sherman tanks (model M4A3) circa 1937-1944 to determine what precise shade of olive drab the tanks were painted. If you're very lucky, they just might happen to have an *authentic* can of the old paint still sitting around that you could buy.

All this so you can take your brand-new plastic model with 45-year-old paint on it and brag about how *authentic* it is. Just be sure you brag about it around your fellow modelers, because nobody else *gives* a flying rat's snout about it.

But of all the hobbies open to us, the one we German/ Americans love most is collecting. Not just hoarding — although we're pretty good at that too — but serious, scholarly, discriminating collecting. Whether we collect "Precious Moments" statuettes or Yam Masks from Papua New Guinea, we're aiming for an *encyclopedic* collection.

What we have here are two such definitive collections, those of Mr. Florian Flugvogel, nationally famous for his wide ties, and Mrs. Delmer (Delia) Etzeldorfer, whose pencil collection has been written up in the Lifestyle sections of three different newspapers.

PENCIL COLLECTION MAY OPEN AS PUBLIC MUSEUM

Mrs. Delmer (Delia) Etzeldorfer poses in front of the pencil collection started in 1931 by her father, Anton Bieberbach.

Far from serving only as a caretaker on such an important collection, Mrs. Etzeldorfer has expanded her father's collection by nearly 27 percent since he willed it to her in 1967.

"All my other brothers and sisters wanted Poppa to will it to them, but none of them would have taken as nice care of it as I did, and Frankie just plain wanted to sell it for whatever he could get! Poppa knew that all along, so he chose *me* to take care of this," Mrs. Etzeldorfer explained. "I sort of figure he lives on in this collection."

Mrs. Etzeldorfer has refurbished the rear bedroom of her home to house the collection, numbering more than 6,397 pencils. She is considering building an annex to display the shorter, sharpened pencils she also has collected over the years.

MORE AWARDS KNOT A PROBLEM FOR WIDE TIE COLLECTOR

Florian Flugvogel of Gnadenhutten, Ohio, proudly shows off 23 wide ties from his wide tie collection numbering more than 125 prize-winning wide ties. He has taken part in wide tie exhibitions and markets throughout Ohio and western Pennsylvania, and has won a significant number of wide tie competitions.

Florian is wearing his favorite wide tie, which was given to him by Dan Rowan of the TV show "Laugh-In." His collection includes wide ties once owned by such celebrities as Milton Berle, Spiro Agnew, Erik Estrada and Charles Bronson during his Flower Power period.

Mr. Flugvogel currently is engaged in a bidding war with Pee Wee Herman for the wide tie Marlo Thomas gave Alan Alda in the wedding scene from the 1969 movie *Jenny*.

In Germany, it is easier to get beer delivered to your home than it is to get home milk delivery. No wonder then that beer bottles come with resealable caps to facilitate the continual sipping process.

Beer and *Gemütlichkeit*

A sk German/Americans why they drink beer, and they'll probably tell you because it's too thin to eat with a fork. Or they might say, "because it's there," or "because I like it."

German/Americans find it impossible to believe that something we like so much could ever hurt us. It wouldn't be fair. It wouldn't be loyal. It wouldn't be German!

Beer makes us jolly, and lord knows, there's no group that needs to lighten up more than we do.

German/Americans are hard-driving, open-throttle people. (There are about as many Type-B German/Americans as there are naturally blond Chinese.) We use beer to slip our pedal-to-the-metal lives into neutral once in a while. Of course, sometimes we downshift a little too fast or too often, and we all know how costly transmission repairs can be.

Gemütlichkeit is the German version of nirvana, a disembodied state of bliss in which one is oblivious to the clamor of the world. While it is possible to reach *Gemütlichkeit* without beer, keep in mind that it's also possible to crawl up on your roof without a ladder. In either case, the problems start when you have to come down.

But *Gemütlichkeit* is more than beer. It's the inane behavior that goes with beer: telling jokes you can't remember, singing sad songs in an ancient male bonding ritual, and trying to solve the riddle of why something called a stein — a stone — seems to get lighter the more you lift it. Maybe this chapter will help solve these mysteries.

Understanding Your Beer Stein

Beer steins are the perfect souvenir to bring home from Germany because they represent a major cultural aspect of German life. As for the other major aspect of German culture, well, sauerkraut-pickling tubs won't fit under an airplane seat.

Virtually every American who has ever gone to Germany has bought a stein. German/Americans who have never gotten closer to Germany than Epcot Center all have one. German/American teetotalers (all seven of them) have one. It shows the world that we're *sehr Deutsch*, and it doesn't keep us awake at night the way a cuckoo clock would.

Now that you've bought a stein, you really should try to understand what it means, culturally and artistically. Here are some answers to the most frequently asked questions about steins.

Why do German beer steins have lids?

Although Germans always have been a very sanitary people, seven-eighths of all German words begin with the letters, "sch..." The more beer people have, the harder it is to pronounce "Sch..." words. You'd want a good heavy lid on your stein too, if you were concerned with basic sanitation.

Lids also keep your close personal friends from drinking from your stein when you leave the room for relief, or when you just plain pass out. If your beer stein does not have a small lock with a digital code known only to you, you have been cheated.

Why are they called "steins"?

"Stein" means "stone" in German, a remarkably modern interpretation of a very old word. The word "stein" was first used in the 14th century, when Alois the Elder, Archbishop of Oberunterulmergauschlosstal wrote to Pope Suburban II, "It is impossible to get anything done around here. The peasants all sit around with tall glasses of beer, getting stoned...."

Other scholars translate the passage to mean, "The peas-

Sanitary lid to prevent exchange of airborne bodily fluids caused by drunks trying to say words beginning in "Sch..."

Somebody's crown, and a dangerous place to get your tongue stuck

Patriotic symbol serving useful function as lid opener

Silly sayings

Loud party with no women present

Oak leaf victor's wreath

Innertube worn as part of uniform

Only two can stay on their horses next morning

Rep tie

Ropes to remind you that military service is not entirely voluntary

This side down

ants are impossible. Because potatoes have not yet been discovered, they sit around eating stones all day" (or "throwing stones at me all day...").

In England, beer is served in what are called "mugs," in reference to the heavy drinker's tendency to see his own face in the bottom of the "mug" and thereby be frightened to death.

Germans, being more patriotic than other peoples, construct their better steins so that you can see the picture of the Kaiser and Mrs. Kaiser in the ceramic bottom. This reminds the average German beer drinker that he has another two years of military service staring him in the face and forces him to order another beer to forget.

What does it say on my stein?

You really don't want to know. In one picture are a bunch of guys in the National Guard wearing innertubes over their uniforms, toasting the Kaiser's health.

The next picture shows all the guys from the regiment whooping it up on leave, throwing their hats in the air, apparently unaware (or perhaps unconcerned) that there aren't any women around to celebrate with.

In the final picture, only half the boys from the party are capable of getting on, or staying on, their horses the next morning when they have to report back to base. It's no wonder they've lost their last three wars in a row.

What are all the decorations on my stein? There are leaves and ropes and all sorts of stuff. Is this symbolism, or what?

Yes, this is all symbolism, and very touching indeed. The leaves bound with ribbons are a victor's wreath, although what you will win if you spend all your time sitting around drinking out of a cup with a cap is uncertain.

The rope symbolized the call of the Fatherland to all of its able-bodied sons to sign up for a good seat in a border skirmish. Most of those 19th-century warlets were fought against the French, because, like the Poles, the French lived close by. Unlike the Poles, however, the French had restaurants worthy of an invasion.

The Germans have always liked to fight but never wanted to get too far away from their hometown brew. This is why the Germans, who are deeply attached to their local beer, never became a major colonial power. Meanwhile, the British, who will drink anything, went everywhere drinking and taking everything they could get their hands on.

OVERLEAF: TROUPE TO GIVE *GEMÜTLICHKEIT* A JUMP-START

Die Kinder der Flasche, a German/American performance art troupe from Cleveland, will perform at the Cincinnati *Oktoberfest* as part of an artistic exchange program between the two cities.

Die Kinder have been performing together since they met while studying mime in Berlin. Explains troupe founder Gail Geiselgastig, "Nothing irritates people faster and more thoroughly than mime, and nobody irritates other people as much or as fast as the Germans. That's why we went to Germany to study mime."

Die Kinder's program will include the critically acclaimed mime piece *Der Höschen Kavalier*, the only known mime piece set to polka. It is the story of a thin young man who goes on a picnic and unpacks his lunch.

Critics have praised its "minimalist action, baroque instrumentation and deep philosophical resonances." Audiences have responded by falling asleep or going out to the lobby to flirt.

"We established *Die Kinder* as a way of proving that German/Americans *can* have a lot of fun, and that we party as hard as we work," says music director Bill Pfaffle. "We thought of calling ourselves the Hilarious Herrs and the Frenetic Frauleins, but it seemed, you know, too American." ▶

Old German Drinking Songs, Translated

For years, German/Americans tried desperately to fit into polite Anglo-American society by adapting old German folk songs into the popular music of the day. What came out of this misguided effort were songs like "My Marzipanny Baby," or "The Lullaby of Bismarck," also known as "The North Dakota Love Theme."

Less popular with a general American audience were songs like "Standing (at attention) on the Corner" and the folk-pop favorite from the 1970s, "When I Can Read Your Mind."

Things eventually got so bad that most Americans thought German/American music consisted entirely of Wayne Newton whining his way through *Danke Schön*, and it was impossible to get anyone to laugh at *Take Me to Your Lieder* jokes.

But German/American music is a rich heritage of polkas, schottishes, ländler, two-steps and, most important, drinking songs.

If you go to a good German/American bar, VFW hall or bowling alley, you can hear authentic German/American drinking songs like the ones below. My experience has been that if you want to hear the singing, you've got to get there by at least 8:30. After that, everybody forgets the words and just hums real loud. By 11, the whole room sounds like what Henry Kissinger would sound like if he had been born as a very large fly.

For the musicologists among us, I would like to offer a quick sampling of some of the more famous German drinking songs.

The first is an old agribusiness song from Lübeck, one of Germany's earliest centers of insider trading in pork bellies futures.

Du, Du, lease me a Holstein,
Du, Du, lease me a bin.
Du, Du, lease me a Holstein,
My fiscal year's ending real soon!
Ja, Ja, Ja, Ja — My fiscal year's ending real soon!

If some songs seem deceptively simple, it's because it's very difficult to remember lots of words when you're drunk. Nevertheless, there usually is a hidden moral behind even the simplest ditty.

Ach, you lover, Augustine, Augustine, Augustine,
Ach, you lover, Augustine, Augustine, Ach!
Swing this way and that way and this way and that way.
Ach, you lover, Augie, bodily fluids are bad.

One of the great strengths of folk music is its ability to comment on the lives of the common people, describing their hopes and their trials. Never mind that they've brought most of these trials down on their own heads. Another trial is a great reason for another round and another song.

This next song is a favorite for those singers already past the denial stage:

THE HAPPY STUMBLER
I love to talk in therapy, about how much I drank.
And as I talk, the guilt it swells, because I really stank.
Valerie Kupferschmidt, where are you,
Don't say no no no no no no, Valerie Kupferschmidt,
This time I will be good.

Some songs are quite recent but still have the feel of antiquity. Then again, some songs sound like they were written by the sort of young snots you wouldn't want to have moving in next door to you.

THE PORK BARREL POLKA
Roll out the suburbs, we'll sell the farm for a song!
Bring on the condos, industrial parks, come along!
Grandfather Ubl, never bought tractors — too new.
We'll show that old crank who's modern,
And we'll get rich too!

4,833 BOTTLES OF BEER ON THE WALL Mr. Edwin Schottelkotte is surrounded by a small portion the 4,833 cans of his award-winning beer-can collection. Started with "just a few leftover cans in 1973," the collection now takes up three-quarters of the basement level of Mr. Schottelkotte's home. "I'm just a lucky guy," Ed says.

Drinking songs long have been exclusively a male domain, but in recent years even the most sodden drunks have noticed that women's role in society has changed. Generally speaking, these old boys *want* these changes for their daughters, but they'd hit the ceiling if their wives ever changed more than the table-cloth.

MS. LILI MARLENE

Underneath the laser, by the new mainframe,
Scanning all her data, each night she is the same;
She hacks for the answer she desires,
She'll get it yet, she has the fire,
She'll be Doctor *Marlene,*
It's Professor Lili, too.
She'll have that doctorate
And the Nobel, well, maybe too.

The Revenge of the Teetotalers

This probably isn't the right place to bring this up. I mean, this *is* a book about Germans, and it *is* the beer chapter, after all, but times and community standards *do* change.

As a society we no longer tolerate drunken drivers, and we recognize that drinking is a disease.

The problem with the disease model is that you have to be so blasted *serious* around the afflicted. You can never make *any* fun of the infirm in our enlightened age.

Far be it from me to hold anyone up to scorn, ridicule and disapprobation, but I think it's time we started taking advantage of social drinkers. Somebody's got to be the focus of society's humor. We need a slow-moving target, and Dan Quayle isn't going to be around forever.

So let's take advantage of the modest social drinker — the one who doesn't drive after more than one glass of wine, and who once or twice a year gets slightly woozy at a party.

Here's a way for teetotalers to get a little revenge for the years of ridicule poured on them by their drinking friends.

Amusing Things to Do to the Tipsy

1. Play Rag Doll. When your partner goes to bed (after taking an aspirin, of course), kneel on the mattress, put your arms around her/him and shake her/him like you shook your Raggedy Ann doll when you were 5. For a complete surprise, wait till she/he begins to doze off.

2. Play Wave Machine. Similar to Rag Doll, except that you lift your partner up suddenly while she/he is lying in bed, and then with equal swiftness, lay her/him back down. Repeat. You may not want to play this game if you don't have a plastic cover under the sheets.

3. Go ice skating. Cold winter air is bracing, which means that you sober up real fast. Your partner will *need* to sober up at warp speed when you start twirling her/him around in figure eights. The other skaters will be vastly amused by her/his expressions and comments.

4. Go to the county fair when your sweetie is full of *Gemütlichkeit* and check out the rides that scare even the teenagers. You can even offer your partner some cotton candy beforehand to make her/his joy complete.

5. Interact with your partner's hangover. Play some records at full blast, particularly Chinese opera, John Cage, Def Lepard or anything with extended drum solos.

6. Check your partner's reaction time by building something that requires lots of nails, or cook something with new and unusual aromas.

7. Buy a tribal mask. After your partner has gone to bed, put on the mask and climb in bed, leaving the bathroom light on. When she/he turns over and sees the mask, growl like the little girl in *The Exorcist*.

8. Put a finger gently on one of your partner's nostrils, then blow lightly across the other to see if you can make a sound like you can by blowing across the top of a beer bottle. Try to play a tune.

VIELE DANK!

A book like this is such a collaborative effort that it seems a little presumptuous to claim authorship all by myself. So I'll just call myself the instigator of this whole thing, and the ringleader of a band of water-walkers who have done so much to make all this possible.

Right at the top of this list comes Adaire Colleen Peterson, the love of my life, my best friend and boon travel companion. I'll go anywhere with you, kid!

New Ulm, Minnesota, America's most German town and the Polka Capital of the Nation (a title I always thought we had won by default) is my hometown and responsible for so much of this book. I hope my friends, teachers, classmates, girlfriends and especially the grown-ups and kids of the South State Street Picnic Association and Rock Pitching Society recognize my continuing affection for them all in this book.

My grandmother, Margaret Strehlau Oas, the Berliner who was definitely not a cream pastry, and who lived in New Ulm with us and all those Bavarians and Bohemians, would be happy to know that I'm finally writing about Germans. I'm still stealing my father's stories about the characters he met daily, and I'm pleased to report that my mother is very proud of me because my earlier Scandinavian book was quoted *from the pulpit* by a Lutheran minister.

Jonathan Lazear is a great agent. Only Congressman Jim Wright can arrange better book deals, and Jonathan's deals don't get investigated. Dan Bial at Harper & Row has been a great help, baffled as he must sometimes have been by my phone calls.

Sylvia Paine, the whiz-bang editor, knows almost as much about baseball as she does about editing. I'm terrified that she'll retire from editing and become an umpire. Sylvia, if you do, you've got to yell "Yer Out!" instead of "Delete!" but otherwise, it's the same. Tara Christopherson's sense of style shows in her art direction for this book, and her sense of style also shows when she doesn't panic when I switch photos on her at the last moment. Tom Casmer designed a Deutschneyland logo that's as jolly and swell as Tom himself.

The cover photo is of Dr. Lowell Weber, my physician, who runs a mean treadmill. Dr. Weber shrugs off his new modeling career as just one more thing an M.D. must do these days to keep his patients happy. I wish I had space to thank all the models by name, some of whom may not want their names known.

The photos in this book wouldn't have been much without the wonderful props. Bonnie "Golden Needles" Carlson is responsible for all the outrageous clerical dickeys. George B. Ryan of United Hospitals and Tom Macht of James Philips Company supplied the medical technology. Dr. Ann Vogel and the New Ulm Heritage Festival are the source of those great morel mushroom costumes. Reynolds Fisher of Terry Feldmann's Imports loaned us the Mercedes, John Lenertz loaned us the office and the Fosses loaned their house for the Bragging Booth photo. The Fosses volunteered themselves, their children and their needlework time and again on this book. Thanks to Lennis Carpentier for sharing his wide ties against his wife's better judgment, Dick and Dianne Lueck for letting me photograph their collections of beer bottles and pencils and Hotel Seville for hosting the Ego Fair picture. And finally, to Joanne Fisher at the University of Minnesota's Swine Research Center, thanks a bundle, but I hope I never have to deal with piglets again in my life.